John James Lias

The Atonement Viewed in the Light of Certain Modern Difficulties

Second Edition

John James Lias

The Atonement Viewed in the Light of Certain Modern Difficulties
Second Edition

ISBN/EAN: 9783744708548

Printed in Europe, USA, Canada, Australia, Japan

Cover: Foto ©ninafisch / pixelio.de

More available books at **www.hansebooks.com**

THE ATONEMENT

VIEWED IN THE LIGHT OF CERTAIN

MODERN DIFFICULTIES.

THE ATONEMENT

Viewed in the Light of Certain
Modern Difficulties.

BEING THE

HULSEAN LECTURES FOR 1883, 1884.

BY THE

REV. J. J. LIAS, M.A.
VICAR OF ST. EDWARD'S, CAMBRIDGE.

Second Edition.

LONDON:
JAMES NISBET & CO., 21 BERNERS STREET.
MDCCCLXXXVIII.

PREFACE TO THE SECOND EDITION.

The sale of a first edition of these Lectures seems to indicate that the want they were designed to supply has been felt. And in truth there is great need just now for a more widespread acquaintance with the true attitude of Christian theology in all ages toward the principle of Atonement. Every assault upon the Christian faith in these days involves an attack upon what is described in these pages as the "Substitution theory." And this theory is not regarded in any sense as a theological outpost. It is represented in all sincerity—for myriads of Christian Divines have so represented it—as the fundamental principle of the Christian faith. It is thus attacked in Mr. Cotter Morison's *Service of Man*, a book which appeared after these Lectures were delivered. "The eternity of hell torments," he says,[1] "is a doctrine discarded by a number of divines, who yet cling to the doctrines of the Incarnation and the Atonement. There is nothing to assure us that, in a hundred years' time, these also will not be discovered to be unscriptural." He admits, however, that "the Christian theology was evolved" during the decline and fall of the Roman empire.[2] Thus the "moral iniquities and obliquities" of which he com-

---

[1] *Service of Man*, p. 35.   [2] Ibid.

plains[1] were not at least the work of Christ and His Apostles. But with regard to the "doctrine of the Atonement," to which he clearly refers,[2] for he describes it as "the centre of the Christian religion," its "moral iniquity and obliquity" must be set down to a period much later still.

That the Substitution theory does suggest grave difficulties to an increasing number of minds is a fact that cannot be disputed. And it is therefore necessary to diffuse as widely as possible the knowledge of the fact that the Christian Church is in no way committed to it. At the same time, it cannot be too emphatically declared that nowhere in these pages will a denial of Substitution as an *element* in redemption be found. Vicarious suffering is the law of the universe, and any system professing to explain the redemption of mankind without reference to it must needs be a failure. This truth has been most distinctly admitted in these Lectures.[3] What has been resisted is the attempt to represent it as the only element in Christ's work of satisfaction for sin. That Christ endured many things to save us from the suffering which is the natural consequence of our sin, is not, cannot be, denied. What is denied is, that the Father's justice or wrath was satisfied by exacting a certain amount of punishment from the Son, and that this punishment was endured by Him in our stead, so as to free us from any liability whatever to any part of such punishment. Such a theory, general as it was, no doubt, half a century ago, has been shown in these pages not only to be contrary to reason, but contrary to the plainest facts. It has been also shown that not only has it no support from the great Divines of the

---

[1] Page 37. [2] Page 38.
[3] See pp. 43, 66–70, 88–90.

PREFACE TO THE SECOND EDITION. vii

Catholic Church, but that all the great Puritan writers, including Calvin and John Owen, have shrunk from the naked statement of a doctrine which their followers have had no hesitation in laying down as the very foundation of all Christian belief. It is of supreme importance at the present time to let men know that however industriously this doctrine has been propagated, neither Scripture nor the Catholic church are responsible for it.

The author has to thank his various critics for the fair and candid way in which his book has been discussed, and to express his obligations to various correspondents for their expressions of opinion. Only one review of a decidedly hostile character has reached the writer. If he refers to it for a moment, it is in order to offer a plea for the more accurate use of language. The reviewer, with a very free use of italics and capitals to mark the horror with which these Lectures have filled him, selects for the expression of his strongest indignation, the statement in page 31, that "the ψυχή" is "the life-principle which man has in common with the animals." That the word "animal" has undergone some deterioration in our modern use of it, is perfectly true. Nevertheless, it may be useful to remember that an *animal* is that which possesses an *anima*, and that *anima* is the equivalent of the Greek ψυχή. If controversialists would but define their terms before beginning their disputes, in most cases controversy would be still-born. To one other review only does the writer wish to refer. A Wesleyan publication, after some discussion of the statements in these Lectures, makes a frank admission that the doctrine of Atonement has often been very rashly stated, and expresses a hope that the teachers of religion will henceforth be more guarded in their expressions. If the perusal of this little book shall lead any teacher of religion to remember that by the use of incautious language he may be throwing serious difficulties in the way of belief, its author will be fully repaid for the labour of writing it.

Since the reprinting of the Lectures was commenced, a similar admission has been made in a still more influential quarter. It occurs in a review of Dr. Westcott's latest work in the *Record* newspaper. For the great authority of Dr. Westcott can henceforth be quoted in distinct corroboration of the principles advocated in these pages. "No support," he says in a volume just published, "remains for the idea that Christ offered in His sufferings sufferings equivalent in amount to the sufferings due from the race of men, or from the elect: no support for the idea that He suffered as a substitute for each man, or for each believer, discharging individually the penal consequences of their actions. No support for the idea that we have to take account for a legal transaction according to which a penalty once inflicted cannot be required again. The infinite value of Christ's work can no longer be supposed to depend upon His capacity for infinite suffering, or upon the infinite value of each suffering of One Who never ceased to be God."[1] The *Record*, while expressing its dissatisfaction with this language, speaks no longer, as it did in its review of these Lectures, of "a plausible, but dangerous attack" on a cardinal doctrine of the Christian faith, but confesses in the following remarkable words, that greater caution is necessary in the manner in which that doctrine is explained. "Undoubtedly the doctrine of substitution can be, perhaps often has been, so stated, that it *ought to be set aside,*" and again, "the idea is often coarsely conceived, and still more coarsely stated." May

[1] *The Victory of the Cross,* pp. 78, 79.

we not hope that the day is near when the infidel lecturer will be deprived of the material for the cheap but most effective sneer by which he is at present able, too often, to laugh Christianity out of court? that the sceptic will no longer inveigh against its fundamental principles as "base and barbarous," as certain to be rejected even by "the most depraved man, in his right mind?"[1]

A few words of explanation may be permitted. It has been thought well to let the Lectures stand as they were delivered. But the words in page 10, "that Jesus Christ bore, as our substitute, the wrath of the Father against sin," had perhaps better run thus: "by bearing, as our substitute, the wrath of the Father against sin, removed that wrath from us, and procured the entire remission of the penalty of sin from each one of us, which we must otherwise have paid." That Christ was *in some sense* our substitute, that the consequences of our sin, which He bore, were *in some sense* the effects of the Divine Wrath against sin, as has been already stated, is not disputed. What has been controverted, is the idea that by such an explanation we have exhausted the Divine Mystery of Redemption.

Again, the "guilt of sin" is stated in one or two places to have been removed by the sacrifice of Jesus Christ. But as Archbishop Magee says (see note 23, on Lect. I.), guilt cannot be conceived of apart from consciousness. And therefore, strictly speaking, the guilt of sin can never be removed. A sinful action once committed cannot be undone, and the sense of its sinfulness, that is, the guilt of it, remains unchanged through all eternity. But though the *guilt* of sin cannot, in the strict sense of the word, be removed, the *imputation* of such guilt may be taken away.

[1] *Service of Man*, p. 38.

In other words, sin may be pardoned. And this is done when, by the Gospel μετάνοια, the mind of the sinner is one with that of Christ concerning sin. This is in a provisional and preliminary sense the case when the sinner places himself by faith in contact with Christ and His redeeming work. The condition of guilt is abolished, the At-one-ment is final and complete, when the believer is fully united in will with the Man Christ Jesus, and through Him with God.

CAMBRIDGE,
July 17, 1888.

PREFACE.

THESE Lectures have been published chiefly because it seemed likely that a short introduction to the study of the doctrine on which they treat might be useful to the theological student, before entering upon larger works, such as Oxenham's *History of the Catholic Doctrine of the Atonement*, the article on the subject in Herzog's *Encyclopædia* (which has lately been translated), the Archbishop of York's *Bampton Lectures*, the Lectures of the Rev. R. W. Dale (of Birmingham), and the still larger and deeper works of Ritschl and of Baur, the former of which has appeared in an English dress.

It has also appeared probable that intelligent laymen who have not much acquaintance with the Classics, might be glad to meet with a hand-book on the subject which demanded no very deep acquaintance with the dead languages, or the technicalities of theology. With this view the majority of passages cited from early authors (those who wrote in Greek especially) have been translated.

The bequest of Dr. Hulse prescribes that the Lectures delivered on his foundation should either be devoted to the exposition and illustration of Holy Scripture, or to strengthening the evidences of the Christian Faith. It is hoped that these Lectures may, indirectly at least, have the latter effect. A certain theory of Atonement, which, though by no means excluded by the language of Scripture, is not laid down in Scripture itself, has been insisted upon as the very key-stone of the Christian Faith. The rejection of this theory has frequently been regarded both by supporters and opponents of Christianity as the rejection of revealed religion. The object of these Lectures is to show that there is no ground whatever for such a supposition; that the theory in question was not propounded by the first preachers of the Gospel, nor by their successors for the next fifteen hundred years, and that it is not accepted by the vast majority of Christians of our own time. Consequently a man may be a very good Christian without believing it, and a very serious hindrance in the way of belief is thus removed.

At the same time, there is no desire in these pages to explain away the words of Scripture. That Christ was a proper propitiation for sin; that He reconciled God to man as well as man to God, that He removed the wrath of God against man for sin, that He made "a full, perfect, and sufficient sacrifice, oblation and satisfaction for the sins of the whole world," is as fully believed by the writer of these pages as by the most ardent advocate of the substitution theory. But he feels that what are called "clear views of the Atonement" are the cause of the utmost perplexity to many. And he believes that there are many who, like himself, find it impossible to stake their faith in Christ on the accuracy of a single theological proposition not to be found in God's Word, and who feel that God Himself only can fully understand the various aspects of so deep, so mysterious, so intricate a problem as the method of Propitiation for man's sin.

Believing that a brief and definite statement of what is *de fide* on this point in the Christian Church is still a *desideratum*, and that at the present time, when so many popular misrepresentations of Christianity are abroad, such a statement is an absolute necessity, the writer has found in this belief an additional reason for venturing into print. While as to the considerations advanced in the last lecture, they are not to be regarded as constituting a theory of the Atonement or anything like it, but simply as a few suggestions illustrative, from various points of view, of a great and Divine mystery surpassing the thoughts of man.

CONTENTS.

LECTURE I.

POPULAR THEOLOGY AND POPULAR OBJECTIONS.

Strict definition impossible in abstract thought—In theology such definition only desirable as is necessary for practical purposes—Scripture full of paradox—Danger of over-definition in theology—Limits of necessary belief—Objections to the doctrine of Propitiation as commonly stated—Doctrine of Owen—of Edwards—Wesley—Simeon—Hare—Pusey—Is this doctrine necessary truth?—Objections of Socinus—Priestley—Carpenter—Martineau—W. R. Greg—Force of these objections admitted by divines of the Anglican Church—Abp. Magee—Dr Jowett—Maurice—Plan of remaining lectures . . . . pp. 1–18

LECTURE II.

SCRIPTURE TEACHING REGARDING PROPITIATION.

Introduction—Origin of Sacrifice—Origin of the Mosaic Sacrifices—Meaning of the Mosaic Sacrifices—Laying on of hands—Consumption by fire—Sacrifices of Propitiation—of Thanksgiving and worship—of Devotion of the heart—Passover—Day of Atonement—Sacrifice of Christ combines the characteristics of all these—Doctrine of New Testament concerning Christ's Sacrifice—Christ a ransom—His Death the offering of His Life—The Representative Death of the human race—The means of uniting mankind—Possesses a cleansing power—A propitiatory Sacrifice—Bears our burden for and with us—Destroys our mortal body—Correction of misconceptions connected with the words Mediator, Atonement, Remission—One-sided expositions of Scripture—Summary of argument . . . . pp. 19–43

LECTURE III.

THEORIES OF PROPITIATION IN THE CHRISTIAN CHURCH.

Clement of Rome—Barnabas—Ignatius—Justin Martyr—Irenæus—Origen—Gregory of Nyssa—Augustin—Athanasius—Gregory of Nazianzus—Chrysostom—Cyril of Alexandria—Anselm—Abelard—Alexander de Hales—Aquinas—Luther—Calvin—Saxon Confession—Augsburg Confession—Helvetic—Synod of Dort—Westminster Confession—Larger and Shorter Catechisms of the Scotch Presbyterian communities—Later Calvinistic doctrine—Roman Church—William Law—Schleiermacher—Irving—Four modern systems of doctrine — Bushnell — Socinian theory — Maurice—McLeod Campbell and Godet—The last system more fully explained—Conclusion . . . . pp. 44–64

LECTURE IV.

THE VARIOUS ASPECTS OF PROPITIATION.

Vastness of the inquiry—Was the Death of Christ penal and vicarious?—Meaning of these words—True of Christ's sacrifice only to a certain extent—The Sacrifice of Christ to be regarded from various points of view—Christ acts with man for God—Explains the position of suffering in this world's economy (1) as regards the world in general, (2) as it affects individuals—Explains God's attitude to sin—Vindicates God's justice by requiring from man an acknowledgment of the true nature of sin—Manifests God's Love—Deals with God on behalf of man—The "Amen of humanity"—An adequate repentance of the whole human race in Christ—Christ identifies Himself with us that we may be one with Him—Christ a perfect Sacrifice for the sins of the whole world—Christ unites us to one another—By death He destroys death and raises us to eternal life—By enduring pain and death for others He displays the true nobleness of humanity—An explanation of the Doctrine of Propitiation required that falls in with our moral and spiritual needs—Objective necessity for Christ's Death—Subjective necessity for it—Conclusion . . . . pp. 65–90

Notes to Lecture I. . . . . pp. 91–108
Notes to Lecture II. . . . . pp. 109–121
Notes to Lecture III. . . . . pp. 122–137
Notes to Lecture IV. . . . . pp. 138–147

LECTURE I.

POPULAR THEOLOGY AND POPULAR OBJECTIONS.

"*Think not that I am come to send peace on earth: I came not to send peace, but a sword. For I am come to set a man at variance against his father, and the daughter against her mother, and the daughter-in-law against her mother-in-law. And a man's foes shall be they of his own household.*"—ST. MATT. x. 34-36.

IT is the characteristic of abstract thought that when followed out to its utmost limits, it almost invariably lands us in the region of paradox. It matters not whether the subject be scientific or practical, metaphysical or theological, if we pursue it into the realms of abstract definition, some contradiction is almost sure to present itself to our minds. Modern philosophy has awakened to this truth. A profound thinker of our day, as he unfolds to us the First Principles of the philosophy he has made so famous, takes care to impress upon us that the things concerning which he invites us to think are ultimately unthinkable.[1] One of the ablest of the Bampton Lec-

[1] Note 1.

turers of the sister University based a remarkable defence of the Christian scheme upon the utter impossibility of forming correct abstract conceptions of God.[1] And both these able and brilliant writers, however much they may differ on other points, are thoroughly agreed upon this fundamental principle. Not only the Being of God, but such self-evident facts as space, time, matter, motion, our own existence and identity, elude our intellectual grasp as soon as they are followed into the sphere of abstract reasoning. Regarded as observed facts, we can and do reason concerning them. Try to form exact definitions of them, and in the end you will invariably be able to reduce that definition to an absurdity.[2]

In the region of abstract thought the philosophers of our own day, at least, are content to confess this truth and make the best of it. In the domain of theology the passion for definition still rages, though with abated force. And in theology at least this passion has frequently taken the form of insisting strongly upon that one side of a truth which presents itself most vividly to the individual, without any regard to those other aspects of truth which, though really complementary to the former, have too often been regarded as contradictory of it. That we can do without definitions is of course impossible. But it has not always been clearly perceived that they should be strictly confined to what is necessary. And it should be further remembered that by "what is necessary," is meant necessary for all practical purposes. We may be tempted to forget that religion, however much it may afford scope for scientific inquiries, is essentially a matter affecting conduct. And so its statements are rather intended to be acted upon

[1] Note 2.   [2] Note 3.

than to be argued about. The endless controversies concerning free-will and Divine foreknowledge, the relation of faith and works respectively to our justification, the respective spheres of authority and reason in the formation of opinion, might have been reduced within an infinitely smaller compass, and have been carried on with far less bitterness, had men discerned the limits within which exact thought was possible or even desirable on such points.

Moreover, every practical truth has its corrective and complement, which, as has been said, is sometimes mistaken for its opposite. This truth is fully recognised in the Scriptures. The writers of the New Testament are not in the slightest degree afraid of the reproach of paradox. A collection of the paradoxes of Scripture would occupy a considerable space. And not the least of them is involved in the text. If there be one characteristic more marked than another of the Saviour's mission, it is that it was a mission of peace. "Peace on earth," sang the angels at His birth.[1] "Peace I leave with you, My peace I give unto you," He said to His disciples just before His Death.[2] "He is our peace," says the Apostle St. Paul, "Who hath made the two one, and hath broken down the middle wall of partition between" the Jew and Gentile.[3] It is the privilege of Christians that "the peace of God, which passeth all understanding, shall keep their hearts and minds through Christ Jesus."[4] And in spite of all this we are told that Christ did not come to bring peace, but a sword; that He came to sunder those who were previously at one, to introduce divisions into private and family life which, but for Him, would never have existed.

[1] Luke ii. 14.   [2] John xiv. 27.   [3] Eph. ii. 14.   [4] Phil. iv. 7.

The ease with which this apparent contradiction may be explained should be a lesson to us to be less impatient than we are of apparent contradictions in subjects of a more mysterious nature—subjects by no means so easy to bring within the scope of the human intellect. The peace Christ came to bring could only be achieved by the subjection of all that was evil in humanity. And the first step towards that subjection was the intensifying the conflict between good and evil in the man himself, and in the world around him. Peace was to be the reward of victory, and no victory is possible without a battle. Such a battle there has been, and such a battle there is still. Nowhere has it raged more fiercely than in the history of religious opinion. The intellect has had its full share in the corruption which has infected man's nature. Applied, in its imperfect unregenerate condition, to the principles of Divine Truth, it of course commenced by misapprehending them. From this, more than any other cause, have our endless religious controversies arisen. And what is of more consequence still, we may fairly attribute much of the revolt against the revelation of God in Christ which we so much deplore in our own day, not to that revelation itself, but to the trappings wherewith human reason has persisted in arraying it. When a doctrine, high and mysterious, transcending the utmost stretch of our faculties, is presented to our minds, its very vastness has a tendency to repel belief. It has proved an irresistible temptation to the human mind to endeavour to dissipate the mystery, and by bringing it down to the level of human capacity to remove the difficulty of embracing it. But this process has invariably ended in suggesting more difficulties than it removed; and it has too often happened that men have been unable to distinguish between Divine Truth itself, and the incrustations with which the human intellect has surrounded it. They have therefore rejected the teaching of Jesus Christ, not because it was false in itself, but because it has been unsatisfactorily explained to them. Two instances of this rationalising tendency stand out perhaps more conspicuously than any others. And it is remarkable that the one is a leading characteristic of Roman, the other of Protestant theology. The first is the doctrine of Transubstantiation, which undertakes to explain Christ's Presence in the Eucharist; the other is that doctrine of Satisfaction for sin which undertakes to make it clear precisely how and why it was that man is said in Scripture to be "justified," "saved," "redeemed" by the Blood of Christ.

To the doctrine of Satisfaction, as taught by Scripture, by the Church, and in the popular theology of Protestant Christendom, it is my desire to invite your attention in these lectures. If it shall prove that many modern objections to Christianity are objections only to the doctrine of Satisfaction as propounded by certain schools of Protestant theology, some very serious hindrances in the way of belief on the part of many earnest minds will have been removed. And be it remembered that no merely traditional teaching, be it Protestant, or be it mediæval, is binding on the conscience of any member of the Church of England or of any Christian man. "Whatsoever is not contained in Scripture, or may be proved thereby," says our Church, " is not to be required of any man as requisite or necessary to salvation."[1] And though we cannot deny that there are propositions which, though not expressly stated in

[1] Art. VI. of the Church of England.

words by the Scriptures, are yet so clearly involved in what Scripture does say that the denial of them leads of necessity to the denial of Divine Truth, yet we are entitled to demand before we assent to such propositions, that this necessity shall be clearly shown to exist. We are bound to believe what Christ and His Apostles taught, and no more. We are not bound to accept such explanations of their teaching as may have satisfied certain individual minds. For it is obviously possible that an explanation which satisfies one mind may offend another. It is a disaster for the faith of Christ when any body of Christians insists on the acceptance of its own favourite explanation of a cardinal doctrine of Christianity. It is worse still, if when Scripture puts before us the outlines of a Divine Mystery, outlines which, though we but dimly discern them from afar, yet fill our heart with reverence and love, man shall step forward with his presumptuous attempts to reduce the Infinite to rule and measure, and demand that we shall accept his explanation of what is beyond the limits of our understanding.

The doctrine of Propitiation for sin is one of the cardinal doctrines of Christianity.[1] For that reason it is naturally one of those which theologians have been most eager to inculcate and to expound. But it is here that very often the intellect of modern times has broken loose from the demands of faith. The doctrine of the Christian Church concerning Satisfaction for sin has been declared by many modern thinkers to be so monstrous, so incredible, that were they to accept the Christian scheme upon every other point, they would have no alternative but to reject it upon this.[2] The object of these lectures will be to

[1] Note 4.   [2] Note 5.

examine the grounds of this rejection; to discover how far these objections relate to the doctrine of Propitiation as taught by the Apostles of Christ, and how far they are due to the manner in which this doctrine has been formulated in later times; how far, in short, the objections are in conflict with God's truth, and how far with man's presentation of God's truth.[1] For it is quite possible to add to the antagonism which must of necessity exist between a Revelation from God and the corrupt heart of man. It is possible to add to that antagonism the further antagonism which exists between one finite mind and another differently constituted. But while we are perfectly justified in desiring to diminish as far as possible the strain which must always be involved in the acceptance of Christianity by a more or less perverted intellect and will, yet we ought not—no, not to gain a million of proselytes,—designedly to explain away one single syllable of God's Word. That any individual mind can possibly hit exactly the happy mean between excess and defect is hardly to be hoped for. But He, Who is merciful and loving to all, is wont to take the will for the deed, to make a large allowance for human infirmity, provided the purpose be one which He approves. And if that purpose be to commend the truth of God to the minds of men, to remove stumbling-blocks out of a brother's way, to exalt the Word of God above the traditions of men, we may be sure that more good than harm will result from the attempt, that the mistakes of the individual will be overruled to the general welfare.

The remainder, then, of this lecture will be devoted to the task of stating what are still the current concep-

[1] Note 6.

tions entertained by the majority of English people concerning the Atoning Work of Christ, and what are the objections most commonly felt to this mode of stating the doctrine. When we have thus seen for ourselves the difficulties men feel on this subject of Propitiation, we may be in a position to examine how far they apply to the Christian scheme itself, and how far only to systems of theology built upon that scheme; how far those who entertain those objections are to be regarded as irreconcilable foes, and how far they should be looked upon as brethren in heart, who have been alienated from us by stumbling-blocks which human infirmity akin to their own has placed in their way.

Nearly two centuries and a half ago the famous John Owen laid down propositions relative to the Death of Christ which have constituted the main features of the doctrine of Propitiation as taught in this country down to our own times. "Christ," he says, "made satisfaction *by undergoing that punishment* which, by reason of the obligation that was upon those for whom He made satisfaction, they themselves were bound to undergo." "When I say the same," he adds, as though he felt that the assertion was not without its difficulties, "I mean essentially the same in weight and pressure, though not in all accidents of duration and the like."[1] A century later, and Jonathan Edwards, the great American theologian, restates Owen's doctrine, accepting its main feature of Predestinarianism, which we are not now concerned to discuss, but modifying very materially its character in regard to the identity of the punishment borne by Christ and ourselves. By Christ's Death, he says, "was finished all that was

[1] Note 7.

required in order to satisfy the threatenings of the law, and all that was necessary to satisfy Divine justice; then the utmost that vindictive justice demanded, even the whole debt, was paid."[1] Again, speaking of Christ's redemptive work, he says, "The first thing necessary to be done is, that this Son of God should become our representative and surety, and so be *substituted in the sinner's room;*" and he adds, "If the Son of God be substituted in the sinner's room, then He comes under the obligation to suffer the punishment which man's sin had deserved."[2] And once more, after enlarging on the reasonableness of a transference of merit from the person accepted to one not so accepted, and of its being viewed as the latter's merit, much as we respect the child or spouse of a friend for that friend's sake, he goes on, "Christ suffered the wrath of God for men's sins *in such a way as He was capable of, being an infinitely holy person, who knew God was not angry with Him personally, but infinitely loved Him.*" And from this point he proceeds to modify Owen's statement very considerably. It was impossible, he says, that Jesus Christ could suffer the torments of the wicked in hell, since the special aggravation of their misery is derived from their knowledge of "God's infinite displeasure towards them, and hatred of them. Christ therefore could bear the wrath of God in two ways only, namely, in having a *great and clear sight* of the infinite wrath of God against the sins of men, and in enduring the *effects* of that wrath." He teaches that at the time of His sufferings Christ had a "clear sight of the dreadful evil and odiousness of sin, and of the dreadfulness of the punishment which He suffered to deliver them."[3] He tries to evade the difficulty which

[1] Note 8. [2] Note 9. [3] Note 10.

his acute and logical mind clearly perceives in the doctrine as taught by Owen and others, by saying that Christ's bearing the burden of our sins may be considered as something diverse from His bearing God's wrath. That bearing God's wrath consisted in the clear apprehension He had of what God's wrath against sin was, and of the tremendous nature of the punishment with which He must needs requite it.

But it is almost a truism to observe that the leaders of thought are almost invariably more cautious, more accurate, more reverent in their language than their followers. The mass of mankind do not perceive the difficulties which are evident to thoughtful men. And so, in spite of Edwards' carefully pondered and measured statement, popular theology has continued to teach that Jesus Christ bore, as our substitute, the wrath of the Father against sin. Even divines of note have accepted the doctrine without question. John Wesley is usually most careful in limiting his statements on this point to the very words of Scripture. Yet he says on one occasion that " God imputes our sins, or the guilt of them, to Christ."[1] Another great religious leader, whose name is still a power in this, his own University, says that " Jesus Christ is our surety and substitute."[2] And again, " If God had forgiven sins without any atonement, His justice, to say the least, would have lain concealed, perhaps we may say would have been greatly dishonoured. But when, in order to satisfy the demands of justice, God sends, not an angel or an archangel, but His own dear Son, and lays on *Him* our iniquities, and exacts of Him the utmost farthing of our debt, then indeed is the justice of God declared, yea,

[1] Note 11. [2] Note 12.

is exhibited in the most awful colours."¹ Such is the teaching of one so justly venerated among us as Charles Simeon.² Another great teacher, whose name is scarcely less honoured among us, is said by a recent sceptical writer —though I cannot find the passage in the work from which it is cited—to have declared that "Christ must suffer for our sins, because God could not forgive sin without punishing it."³ The great theologian of the sister University, Dr. Pusey, in some of his later writings, lays very great stress on the necessity of the doctrine that Christ suffered in our stead. "The doctrine," he says, "that Christ made amends to the justice of God by taking our place, is plainly contained in every place of Scripture which speaks of the vicariousness of His Death, or our redemption by His Blood." "Any statement of vicariousness or atonement or redemption involves what is meant by satisfaction to the Divine justice, that what was justly due to our sins Christ paid, the punishment we justly deserved, Christ bore." And he explains the objections to this doctrine which have found favour of late, by the influence upon modern thought of Milton's *Paradise Lost*, and of the unconscious denial of the Divinity of Christ which pervades the whole of that noble poem.⁴

It is not my purpose to controvert this doctrine. If it bring satisfaction and comfort to any man, far be it from me to try and deprive that man of his satisfaction. But there are minds to which this doctrine not only brings no satisfaction or comfort whatever, but it causes them the utmost perplexity and disquiet; nay, it even drives them to reject the whole Gospel of Christ.⁵ The question there-

¹ Note 13.   ² Note 14.   ³ Note 15.
⁴ Note 16.   ⁵ Note 17.

fore arises, not whether this explanation be in itself a rational and tenable explanation of the language of Holy Scripture on this high and mysterious subject, but whether it be the only rational and tenable explanation of that language. The question arises, whether it be possible to hold firmly to the truth that Jesus Christ was a true and proper Sacrifice for sin, that we were redeemed, saved, justified by His Blood; that on the Cross He offered Himself as a full, perfect, and sufficient sacrifice, oblation and satisfaction for the sins of the whole world, that He bare our sins in His Own Body on the tree, without being compelled to acknowledge that all this was effected by His having borne the Wrath of God against sin, or an exact equivalent to it, in our stead; that it was His having borne the punishment of our sins which satisfied the insulted dignity of the Father, paid the penalty inexorably demanded by His justice, and so enabled Him to lay His wrath aside. The question is a vital one for our own age. For they are no carping or sneering sceptics, but souls deeply in earnest, who have failed to see how the justice of God can be vindicated by punishing the innocent and letting the guilty go free. They are no hardened scoffers who have been unable to discern why the Divinity of Christ should depend on the theory that an infinite offence can only be expiated by an infinite penalty. And yet, on the other hand, a Christianity without Propitiation is no Christianity at all. It is not even common morality. A general amnesty to offenders who have never comprehended the gravity of their offence is a simple invitation to offend again. It is only when the majesty of law is duly recognised that pardon can be granted. If, then, we can show that it is not the Scripture doctrine of Propitiation that is at fault, but that the centre of gravity of the Christian scheme has been shifted by modern theories of the Atonement, if we can show that satisfaction to Divine justice has taken the place of the Restoration of the Divine Image in fallen man, that the doctrine of Propitiation rests upon that of Christ's Godhead, and not Christ's Godhead upon the necessity of exacting an adequate penalty either from the offender or his substitute, if we can persuade men that Christ's Incarnation, not His Death, has been from the first the pivot upon which the Gospel scheme has revolved, we may perhaps do something to restore that faith which has so unhappily been lost.

Faustus Socinus seems to have been the first to have boldly rejected what in his day was rapidly coming to be the received doctrine on this point.[1] His followers have stated their objections with great clearness. Priestley for instance, in his "History of the Corruptions of Christianity," thus propounds his view of what he considers the corrupt doctrine of the Atonement: "It is connected with the doctrine of the Divinity of Christ, because it is said that sin, as an offence against an *infinite being*, requires an *infinite satisfaction*, which can only be made by an *infinite person*, that is one who is no less than God himself. Christ therefore, in order to make this infinite satisfaction for the sins of men, must himself be God, equal to the Father. The justice of God being now fully satisfied by the death of Christ, the sinner is acquitted. Moreover, as the sins of men have been thus imputed to Christ, His righteousness is, on the other hand, imputed to them, and thus they are accepted of God, not on account of what they have done themselves, but for what Christ has done for them." This

[1] Note 18.

doctrine he " conceives to be a gross misrepresentation of the character and moral government of God."[1] His disciple, Carpenter, takes exception to the doctrine of the Atonement as taught in his day, on the ground that it represents the Death of Christ as " a SATISFACTION *to the justice of God,* and the PROCURING CAUSE *of divine mercy,* inasmuch as it was necessary to remove some obstruction which antecedently existed to the exercise of it."[2] It is undeniable, however, that these writers, in their recoil from propositions which they considered untenable, have gone so far as to explain away as figurative the most distinct statements of Holy Scripture, and that with this they have coupled an absolute repudiation of the doctrine of the Divinity of Jesus Christ.

A later writer, who, equally with Priestley, and it may be presumed for similar reasons, has rejected the belief in the Divinity of Christ, thus eloquently states the doctrine of substitution, as it presents itself to him : " The Being who hangs upon that Cross is not man alone; but also the everlasting God, who created and upholds all things, even the sun that now darkens its face upon Him, and the murderers that are waiting for His expiring cry. The anguish He endures is not chiefly that which falls so poignantly on the eye and ear of the spectator; the injured human affections, the dreadful momentary doubt; the pulses of physical torture, doubling on Him with full or broken wave, till driven back by the overwhelming power of love disinterested and Divine. But He is judicially abandoned by the Infinite Father; who expends on Him the immeasurable wrath due to an apostate race, gathers up into an hour the lightnings of Eternity and

[1] Note 19. [2] Note 20.

lets them loose upon that bended Head. It is the moment of retributive justice; the expiation of all human guilt: that open brow hides beneath it the despair of millions of men; and to the intensity of agony there, no human wail can give expression. Meanwhile, the future brightens on the elect; the tempests that hung over their horizon are spent. The vengeance of the lawgiver having had its way, the sunshine of a Father's grace breaks forth, and lights up, with hope and beauty, the earth which had been a desert of despair and sin. According to this theory, Christ, in His death, was a proper expiatory sacrifice; He turned aside, by enduring it for them, the infinite punishment of sin from all past and future believers in this efficacy of the cross; and transferred to them the natural rewards of His own righteousness. An acceptance of this doctrine is declared to be the prime condition of the Divine forgiveness; for no one who does not *see* the pardon can *have* it. And this pardon, again, this clear score for the past, is a necessary preliminary to all sanctification; to all practical opening of a disinterested heart towards our Creator and man. Pardon, and the perception of it, are the needful preludes to that conforming love to God and men, which is the true Christian salvation." [1]

It must be confessed that this, though coming from an Unitarian source, is a fair statement of the doctrine which has found such wide acceptance among Christians of the Reformed communions. Let us now add, from an avowed, but earnest and candid sceptic, lately removed from us by death, an expression of the objections to which he conceives that theory to be liable. He speaks of the " strangely inconsistent doctrine that God is so just that

[1] Note 21.

He could not let sin go unpunished, yet so unjust that He could punish it in the person of the innocent." "It is for orthodox dialectics," he adds, "to explain how the Divine Justice can be *impugned* by pardoning the guilty, and yet *vindicated* by *punishing* the innocent."[1] The force of these objections has been owned by members of our own communion, who have not hesitated to sanction and restate them. Archbishop Magee, in his work on the Atonement, a work whose orthodoxy has never, so far as I know, been disputed, has, in a very remarkable manner, avoided committing himself to many of the propositions to which exception had been taken by Unitarian writers.[2] "The doctrine of the Atonement," says an eminent living thinker and scholar, "has often been explained in a way at which our moral feelings revolt. God is represented as being angry with us for what we never did. He is ready to inflict a disproportionate punishment on us for what we are. He is satisfied by the sufferings of His Son in our stead. Christ is a victim laid on the altar to appease the wrath of God. He is further said to bear the infinite punishment of infinite sin. When He had suffered or paid the penalty, God is described as granting Him the salvation of mankind in return."[3] And another deep thinker, and late Professor at our own University, thus formulates his objections to the current theology of thirty years back. "They say," he writes, "Christ came to deliver sinners from sin. This is what the sinner asks for. Have we a right to call ourselves orthodox if we change the words, and put penalty of sin, for sin? Those who say the law must execute itself, must have its penalty, should remember their own words. How does

[1] Note 22. [2] Note 23. [3] Note 24.

it execute itself, if a person, against whom it is not directed, interposes to bear its punishment?" And again, "How, then, can we tolerate for an instant that notion of God which would represent Him as satisfied by the punishment of sin, not by the purity and graciousness of the Son?" And he goes on—"We solemnly abjure all schemes and statements, however sanctioned by the arguments of divines, however plausible as implements of declamation, which prevent us from believing and proclaiming that in the Cross all the wisdom and truth and glory of God were manifested to the creature, that in it man is presented as a holy and acceptable sacrifice to the Creator."[1]

It is not my purpose at present to express any opinion upon these utterances. I propose in the next lecture to examine the words of Scripture, that we may discover precisely what those words do, and what they do not, call upon us to believe in God's Name. Next, I propose to take a brief glance at the history of Christian opinion on this point, that we may know how far the doctrine which has now been stated, and to which, as we have seen, exception has been taken, may be regarded as authoritative and Catholic;—that is to say, how far it may be regarded as having been taught, to use the well-known definition, "semper, ubique, et ab omnibus."[2] When we have ascertained this, we may be in a position, not to lay down a

---

[1] Note 25.

[2] I must explain that I take "ab omnibus" to mean "by all *Churches*," not by all individuals, which would reduce the definition to an absurdity. There is scarcely anything whatever which no one has been found to controvert. But it is not so very difficult to ascertain what has been regarded as authoritative by Christian Churches in all ages and in all parts of the world.

B

satisfactory theory of the Atonement, which were a hazardous undertaking, but to understand precisely what Scripture and the Church have laid down on the matter; to understand precisely what is to be believed as requisite and necessary to salvation. And if we find the result to be, that we must leave many utterances of Scripture unexplained and mysterious, shall we, I would ask, my brethren, be any the worse for the discovery? Can we expect that each one of us, while here below, shall be able to compass and comprehend the vastness of that Divine purpose which, as we learn, is beyond the comprehension of the angels in heaven?[1] Will it be surprising if the manifold and many-hued[2] wisdom of God should also prove to be many-sided, and that one side or other of the complex scheme of redemption shall commend itself to men, according to their disposition, their circumstances, their training? If we should arrive at the conclusion that the Atonement made for our sins by Christ is not easy, but hard to explain; that it opens up on every side problems which concern themselves with all the various elements of our humanity, and eventually lose themselves in the Infinite profundity of the Divine Essence, will this be a reproach to the soundness of our theology? Will it not rather prove that we are true disciples of Him of Whom we are taught, "As the heavens are higher than the earth, so are My ways higher than your ways, and My thoughts than your thoughts"?[3]

[1] Eph. iii. 10; 1 Pet. i. 12.   [2] Eph. iii. 10.
[3] Isa. lv. 9.

LECTURE II.

SCRIPTURE TEACHING REGARDING PROPITIATION.

" Wherewith shall I come before the Lord, and bow myself before the high God? Shall I come before Him with burnt offerings, with calves of a year old? Will the Lord be pleased with thousands of rams, or with ten thousands of rivers of oil? Shall I give my first-born for my transgression, the fruit of my body for the sin of my soul?"—MICAH vi. 6, 7.

THE question upon which we shall next enter is the Scripture doctrine of Propitiation. We shall endeavour first to inquire what was the meaning of the sacrifices of the Old Testament, and how far, in their origin, in their significance, and in the ceremonial which accompanied them, they are calculated to throw light upon the Sacrifice of Christ. And next, we shall inquire into the specific statements of the New Testament regarding that Sacrifice. We shall endeavour to ascertain what Scripture does, and what Scripture does not say upon this point, and thus to discover what, in a matter of such consequence, it is actually necessary for us to believe, and what, though it may be regarded as a legitimate deduction from Scripture, is nevertheless to be looked upon as a conclusion of human reason from its utterances, and may therefore, while it is received with respect as a contribution to the elucidation of the subject, be set aside, after full consideration, by those who find themselves unable to accept it, without any derogation to the Divine authority of Revelation. And I may here be allowed to add that in admitting the possibility of human additions to revealed truth on this particular point having come to be believed as though they were that revealed truth itself, I am but treading in the steps of theologians of unimpeached orthodoxy, who have occupied, in the sister University as in this, the position of public lecturers on behalf of revealed religion. Five years before the end of the last century, Dr. Veysie, as Bampton Lecturer at Oxford, affirmed his conviction that much which was taught as the Scripture doctrine of Atonement was in fact only man's deduction from God's truth.[1] And Mr. Benson, one of my predecessors in the post I now occupy, when dealing with a subject closely connected with that which now occupies us, uttered some weighty words of warning against the danger of "teaching for doctrines the commandments of men."[2] The present Archbishop of York, in his Bampton Lectures on the Atonement, has also deprecated the tendency to speculation and dogmatism on this mysterious subject.[3]

Before entering upon the Scripture doctrine of Sacrifice, it seems not unreasonable to say a few words on the origin of Sacrifice itself. Among all the nations of antiquity we find the practice. It consisted, not merely in offering of

---

[1] Note 1.   [2] Note 2.
[3] See Note 25, Lect. 1.

their substance, but in consuming by fire the body of a living being, slain on or at the altar, as an offering to deity. In some cases that living being was a human being. We naturally ask, To what causes can this sacrificial worship be referred? And, as usual, we meet with many explanations of the phenomenon.[1] One supposes that God was conceived of as a kind of magnified man, who took the same kind of pleasure in the consumption of the animal that we should do in partaking of it as food. Another contends that the animal's blood, being the psychic, or sensual principle of life, is actually the very principle of that sin which is inseparably connected with this psychic, or sensual principle, and that thus, the offering of the principle of sin by the shedding of blood is a real, and not a fancied, propitiation for sin, since it is the destruction of that in which sin consists. A third insists that the victim was strictly substituted for the offender, and that the satisfaction for sin was of the nature of what we call a vicarious substitution. A fourth is content to regard the whole act as symbolical, and to regard the animal as the representative of what the man felt to be owing by himself to God.[2] We have no time to enter into a discussion of this question. But we may fairly assume that no one of these particular theories is so conclusively established as to be absolutely beyond dispute. We may therefore regard any one of them as a fair and reasonable explanation, though of course by no means the only fair and reasonable explanation of the facts. The view, therefore, that the ancient sacrifices were originally acts of devotion to God, manifestations of a desire to give our very best to Him to Whom we owe everything, endeavours to express, to the

---

[1] Note 3.   [2] Note 4.

utmost of our power, our inner sense of gratitude and reverence, is a tenable theory. That a conscience burdened with sin should desire to give up its best to propitiate a deity who was believed to be offended, is likewise reasonable. That one who had some particular object in view, on which he had set his heart, should strive to conciliate the good will of the Disposer of events by the offering of all that was dearest in his eyes, is, again, in no degree unnatural. Even the human sacrifices of heathen nations, with the exception of those gloomy rites in which the deities were supposed to derive satisfaction from the spectacle of human suffering—even these human sacrifices may have meant no more than this, that the urgency of the occasion demanded a greater gift than usual; that the offerer who desired the good-will of Deity should prove *his* good-will in return by offering that which to him was the best and dearest thing he had in the world. And the self-dedications of mythical heroes like Curtius, and real ones like Decius, seem to have derived their inspiration from the belief that the moral beauty of the sacrifice was great in the eyes of the gods. Even the heathen conscience could feel that its deities were moved to admiration by an embodiment in act of a sentiment to which humanity instinctively responds. That it was the sacrifice—to use the word in a sense which, if not technically accurate, is by no means unusual—the sacrifice of the best one has, and no idea of substitution, which sometimes weighed with a man even in the offering of a living being, seems clear from the words of the king of Moab which I have taken for my text. Amid the "calves of a year old," the "thousands of rams" which he is ready to offer, comes "ten thousands of rivers of oil." This fact tells us that even in the climax to which his distress and perplexity lead him, even in the proposal to give the fruit of his body for the sin of his soul, he is not moved by any idea of making the life of any creature, even that of his first-born, a substitute for himself, but simply by the hope that he may propitiate the wrath of the unseen powers by the surrender of that which is most precious in his sight. The sacrifice is valuable only as a measure of his sense of the greatness of his transgression, and of his willingness to make every reparation in his power or it.

If this were the primitive belief, it is quite intelligible that, in the course of years, a symbolical meaning may have come to be added. The slain animal may have been held to represent the worshipper, and its death may have served to show forth the truth before God and man that in that worshipper's belief his life were justly forfeit for his sin, and may have been regarded as the figurative offering of that life to God. This additional idea may have attached to sacrifice, and even yet there may have been no thought in the worshipper's mind that the death of the victim was a substitute for his own.

We proceed to a view of the Mosaic sacrifices, and what is involved in them. And here, on the threshold of our inquiry, we find ourselves met with the question whether the offering of living sacrifices was enjoined by Jehovah from the very first—whether it was a command obeyed by Abel, and set at naught by Cain—or whether these sacrifices were the result of the idea to which we have already referred, that the goodness of the giver required an acknowledgment by the sacrifice of the best of his gifts. It may suffice here to say, with my predecessor in the post to whom reference has been already made, that we have no evidence whatever on this particular point beyond the conclusions of human reason. And we may do well to ponder his warning not to be too eager in rushing to conclusions. "Surrounded as we are," he says, " by men anxious to discover and able to detect our very smallest deviation from the essential rules of right reasoning, and to turn the mistakes of the advocates of the Bible into an argument against its inspiration, we never can be too careful of the positions we assume, or the means by which we explain or defend the difficulties of Scripture."[1]

We will, therefore, not encumber our argument with any theory about the human or the Divine origin of sacrifice. We may content ourselves with saying that even though no Divine injunction prescribed it, an universal and spontaneous production of the human heart in its yearnings towards God could be little less than Divine in its origin, could be little less than a foreshadowing of that consecration of the whole principle of sacrifice which took place on Calvary, and that we may find here a justification of the profound remark of Bishop Butler,[2] that it is to the Cross of Christ that we should look for an explanation of the sacrifices of the ancient world, rather than endeavour to find an explanation of *it* in *them*.

Our examination of the principles involved in the Mosaic sacrifices must of necessity be very brief and general. They may be divided into three great classes; first, the ordinary sacrifices of the law; second, the great Feast of the Passover; and third, the ceremonies of the great Day of Atonement. The ordinary sacrifices have been divided into three classes, Propitiatory, Eucharistic or Impetratory, and Devotional. In all these cases the victim was slain by the offerer, at the door of the tabernacle

[1] Note 5.   [2] Note 6.

of the congregation. In each case, with the single exception of the trespass offering, he laid his hands upon the victim before slaying it. The remainder of the ritual differed, as we shall see, in each particular case. It is, of course, impossible to enter into any detailed arguments as to the meaning of each particular ceremony. Every conceivable view has once more found its supporters and opponents.[1] We can but state what appears to be, on the whole, the most satisfactory explanation of the facts. Of the slaying of the victim we shall speak presently. Of the laying on of hands it may suffice to say this much, that no more can be proved out of Holy Scripture than that it was a symbolical act, indicative of the fact that the worshipper regarded the victim as typifying himself, and the attitude he desired to assume towards God. That it involved any substitution of any kind; that the offerer supposed the victim to be in any way appeasing the wrath of God by bearing a punishment which he himself deserved to bear, is nowhere expressly asserted, or even implied in the Jewish Scriptures. It is only one out of various ways of explaining the mysterious rites of the Jewish law of sacrifice.[2] One other point must be noticed—the consumption of the whole or part of the sacrifice by fire. Various interpretations have, as usual, been placed upon this feature of the rite.[3] It is not necessary to adopt any one of them to the exclusion of the rest. It is quite possible that the typical significance of the Mosaic ritual was very extended in its nature, and that it is by no means to be exhausted by any one particular interpretation. But in the use which is made of fire in the Jewish sacrifices, three points seem to be singled out for special notice. First, the victim was given to God; and

[1] Note 7.   [2] Note 8.   [3] Note 9.

the consumption, in some cases of the whole victim, in others of some of its choicest parts, typifies the entire surrender of our best to God. Next, the fact that the ordinary word for burning [1] is never used of consumption on the altar, but that is employed instead which is used also for the smoke of incense,[2] implies that the smoke of the sacrifice, as it mounted up to heaven, signified the ardent desire of the human heart to raise itself to God. And thirdly, it seems reasonable to suppose that the fire itself may have symbolized the intense fervour of love which should animate the worshipper, the reflex of the nature of Him to Whom all worship is directed.

We proceed to a more detailed review of the various kinds of sacrifice. Of the first, or propitiatory sacrifice, the sin and trespass offering is the expression. Much has been written concerning the distinction between the sin offering and the trespass offering.[3] But the Book of Leviticus appears to regard the former as a propitiation for sins committed through ignorance, and the latter as a propitiation for guilt. A certain amount of guilt attached even to sins of ignorance. Consequently, as it would seem, an additional sacrifice beside the offering for his sin or error[4] was required of the transgressor. In the sin offering, as in the remainder of the burnt sacrifices, the hands were laid upon the victim, it was slain "before the Lord," and its blood was sprinkled[5] upon the horns of the altar, and the part which was not consumed upon the altar was, in the most important cases, carried without the camp and burned

---

[1] שרף.   [2] הקטיר.   [3] Note 10.

[4] חטאת signifies, like ἁμαρτία, a *missing of the mark*. Cf. Lev. iv. 2, nd v. 17, 19.

[5] Or, rather, *smeared*. See Kurz, p. 215.

there.[1] The trespass offering, which involves actual moral guilt,[2] is atoned for, it will be found, by the priest,[3] thus typifying the truth that man is unable of himself to make amends for the evil he has done. The burning of the bullock without the camp in the sin offering would seem to signify the removal of the guilt from the congregation of God's people; the eating of the sacrifice by the priest, who was at once the representative of God and man, may either have signified the reconciliation between God and man, or the imparting to the priest, as a representative of the offerer, the condition of acceptance which belonged to the accepted offering, or, in the view that the victim without blemish was regarded as holy to the Lord,[4] it may have meant that the holiness of the victim passed over to the offerer, represented by the priest.[5] It is with diffidence that even these alternative explanations are suggested. Almost every conceivable theory has been broached and defended upon every conceivable point in the Mosaic law,[6] and it is impossible to decide between them.

We come next to the peace, or, as some prefer to call them, the thank offerings. In these the ritual is the same

---

[1] Lev. iv. 12, 21. The same was the case with the ashes of the daily offering, Lev. vi. 9, 11. But in the case of the sin offering the bullock only, the offering of the priest or of the whole congregation, was burned without the camp. In the case of the individual, his offering of a kid was dealt with like the peace offering. See Lev. iv. 26, 35.

[2] Note 11.

[3] Lev. v. vi. See especially vi. 30.

[4] Lev. x. 17.

[5] Or the explanation may be yet more simple. As the office of atonement belonged to the priest, the flesh of the slaughtered animal may have been given to him to do as he pleased with. The trespass offering was eaten solemnly as a part of the ritual. Lev. vi. 29, vii. 6.

[6] Note 12.

as the former, save in the matter of the consumption of the sacrifice. Here a portion of the best is offered by fire to God, a recognition, no doubt, of the fact that we owe our best to Him, while the remainder is eaten by the offerer.[1] Whether we regard the peace offering as a recognition of past, or a supplication for future, favours, we may reasonably look upon the eating of the flesh of the victim by the offerer as a token of his oneness with God. And without forgetting that the priests had no inheritance like the rest of the Israelites, and therefore were intended to "live of the sacrifices," we may be allowed to suppose that there may have been a symbolical meaning in the priest's share of the victim, and that the priest, representing as he did the whole nation in its religious aspect, typified in his eating the sacrifice the share which the whole community had in the well-being of each of its members. The burnt offering, obviously from its position in the Book of Leviticus the most important of all,[2] presents the simplest ritual. Burned whole upon the altar, it expressed the fact that the whole man, body, soul, and spirit, in thought, word, and deed, ought to be offered up a complete sacrifice to the Lord.[3]

The institution of the Passover embodies, in one rite, the idea of all the three sacrifices of which we have just spoken. The Lamb slain solemnly before the Lord; the blood, no longer, we must suppose, after the arrival of the

---

[1] Lev. iii. 1-17, vii. 11-19, xxii. 29, 30. The breast and the shoulder were reserved for the priest (Lev. vii. 31, 32, 34), not ritually, but as a means of subsistence. See Numb. xviii. 8-24; Josh. xiii. 14, &c.

[2] "Das allgemeinste und bedeutendeste Opfer." Tholuck on the Epistle to the Hebrews. Beilage II.

[3] Lev. i. 1-17.

chosen people into their land, sprinkled upon the lintel and two door-posts, as at the original institution, but offered no doubt by sprinkling upon the altar; the consumption of the whole of the flesh of the sacrificed victim, combine in one view all the aspects of the Mosaic sacrifices.[1] And in the ceremonies of the Day of Atonement[2] we have these same characteristics again gathered up in one set of ceremonies, but from another point of view. The one goat is offered up as a representation of the one Great Propitiatory Sacrifice, the other is solemnly set apart as a type of the separation effected by sin. As the body of the animal offered as a propitiatory sacrifice for sin was burned without the gate, so the scape-goat was first laden with the iniquity of the people, and then sent away into the wilderness, thus typifying the idea expressed in the words of Isaiah in reference to those who have not repented of their sin : " Your sins have separated between you and your God, and your sins have caused Him to hide His face from you, that He will not hear."[3] The eternal separation between sin and God is thus proclaimed to us; the utter impossibility of reconciliation between the two, and the absolute necessity, therefore, that the sinner should put away his sin, unless he desires to be sundered for ever from the Lord. Yet I would not be supposed to deny that there is a sense in which, as the author of the very early writing attributed to the Apostle Barnabas teaches, the scape-goat was a type of Christ. In so far as He took on Himself—as He did take on Himself—the burden and punishment of our sins ; in so far as He condescended to become a curse for us ; in so far as He thus identified Himself with suffering

---

[1] Exod. xii. ; Numb. ix. 1-5.
[2] Lev. xvi., xxiii. 27-32; Numb. xxix. 7-11.   [3] Note 13.

and even with sinning humanity, so far the scape-goat was a type of Christ. A type of Christ, because, among other reasons, the sufferings and death of Christ were unquestionably endured to manifest to us how great the burden of sin is; how awful the separation it makes between the soul and God.

One general remark we will make on the Jewish sacrifices before passing from the subject. All the various kinds of sacrifices of slain animals were types of the one Offering on Calvary. That offering, therefore, cannot be regarded exclusively from one point of view, but must combine the characteristics of all.[1] The entire devotion of the unblemished Life of Jesus Christ is typified by the burnt offering; the vital union between Himself and us, by the peace offerings; the full propitiation made for sin, by the sin and trespass offerings; and all by the ceremonies of the Passover and the Day of Atonement. And it is most important to observe that we are not without an intimation that it is the life, and not the death, of the victim which is so well-pleasing to God; that its death is but the mode by which its life is offered. "For the life of the flesh is in the blood, and I have given it you upon the altar to make an atonement (literally to cover upon) for your souls; for it is the blood that maketh atonement (or covereth) for the soul."[2]

Let us now inquire how the doctrine of Propitiation is represented to us in the New Testament. We shall find that not a simple but a very complex idea is there presented to us. The first idea is contained in the words "redemption," "ransom," "price," "buying," all of which are used of the process whereby we are reconciled

---

[1] Note 14.   [2] Lev. xvii. 11. See Note 15.

to God. And they all implied that something was offered to God on our behalf, and even in our stead, by One in every way qualified to do so. In our stead, I say, because our Lord Himself speaks of His being a λύτρον ἀντὶ πολλῶν,[1] and St. Paul speaks of His having given himself as an ἀντίλυτρον on behalf of all.[2] The meaning of the preposition ὑπέρ, the one ordinarily used of the process of redemption, cannot, of course, be pressed either way. It may mean "instead of," or it may not. And if we insist that it does mean "instead of," the question arises why it is used instead of ἀντί, which expresses that idea more distinctly.[3] In three places, however, our Lord is plainly declared to have offered Himself instead of us. But it may be observed, that it is not said in what way He offered Himself in our stead. Nothing is said here of His having borne the Father's wrath against us, or of His having satisfied the Father's justice by bearing our punishment. All that is stated is, that He—He Himself—is the price paid instead of us. But the price itself is definitely stated. In one of the passages already quoted it is His Life which is distinctly stated to be the ransom; that is, the ψυχή, or life principle which man has in common with the animals, not, be it observed, the immortal ζωή, inseparable from Himself, which He came to give to the world.[4] That is what is meant by redemption through His Blood. The blood is the life of man; Redemption by Christ's Blood is redemption by the offer of His Human Life. It was

---

[1] Matt. xx. 28; Mark x. 45.
[2] 1 Tim. ii. 6. See Note 16.   [3] Note 17.
[4] It is impossible to avoid seeing how seriously the indefiniteness of the English language on these points interferes with the endeavour to construct a philosophic theology for the English people.

the offer of that life, the life of a spotless human victim upon the altar of the Cross, which constituted the price paid for our sins. And we are elsewhere informed that our justification has been effected δι' ἑνὸς δικαιώματος— through the setting right of what had been wrong, as though the price paid for us were the pure and perfect Life in the place of the impure, sin-stained lives, and not any punishment whatsoever, however necessary it might be to the completeness of the offering that such punishment, or rather suffering, should be endured. It is a remarkable fact, whatever be its significance, that we are never in Scripture directly said to be redeemed by the Death of Christ, but always by His Blood. Reconciled, on one occasion, we are said to be by the Death of Christ, though even then it is added, "Much more, being reconciled, we shall be saved by His Life."[1] But it would seem as though the price paid by Christ on our behalf was His Life, not His Death. In one place, it is true, we are told that Christ redeemed us, or bought us out of the power of an enemy, by becoming a curse for us.[2] And we are repeatedly told that He died for us, for our sins, for the ungodly.[3] And yet it is, as I have said, remarkable that when the price is mentioned, it is always declared to be the Blood or Life of the sacrificial victim, not His Death.[4]

---

[1] Rom. v. 10. Cf. Eph. ii. 13-16, where the death of Christ is said to be the slaying of the enmity between God and man, not the price paid for our redemption. Also Rom. vi. 6.

[2] Gal. iii. 13. Cf. 2 Cor. v. 21, where, however, ἁμαρτία, the translation of the Hebrew חטאת, clearly means a sin offering.

[3] Rom v. 6, 8; 1 Cor. xv. 3; 2 Cor. v. 14, 15; 1 Thess. v. 10; Heb. ii. 9.

[4] Note 18.

There is one passage[1] in which the work of redemption is closely connected with the death of Christ. But it does not contain the phrase "through" His Death, as we have elsewhere διὰ τοῦ αἵματος αὐτοῦ. The distinction may be a fine-drawn one, but it is also possible that something may be meant by it. The passage is that in which the necessity of Death is insisted upon by the figure of a testament which has no validity until the death of the testator has taken place (that is, if the proper translation of διαθήκη be testament and not covenant here).[2] The power of the Blood of Christ to purge our sins has just been asserted, in the usual language. And then before introducing the figure of the testament and the testator, the Sacred Writer proceeds, "And for this cause He is the mediator of the New Testament in order that, death having taken place unto the redemption of the transgressions that were under the first testament, they that have been called might have the promise of the eternal inheritance." The whole meaning rests here upon the force of the preposition εἰς. It may either mean that Christ's death was a necessary step in the process of redemption, or it may mean that Christ's Death took place in order to effect that redemption. But even if we accept the latter explanation we might conclude, both from the analogy of the ancient sacrifices, and from the universal use of the word "Blood" in preference to "death" in every single passage but this one, that it was not the enduring the punishment of death as a satisfaction of the Father's wrath, but the offer on the Cross, through death, of His unblemished Life to God, which constituted the main ground of the efficacy of Christ's Sacrifice.

[1] Heb. ix. 15.   [2] Note 19.

We come next to another class of passages which have a deep significance. The well-known passage in the 2nd Epistle to the Corinthians [1] may, according to the idiom of the New Testament, be rendered either, as in the Authorized Version, "then were all dead," [2] or according to the Revised Version, "then all died." If the latter, then one point in the Death of Christ was that the Death of the One Representative Man was in a sense the death of all humanity. This interpretation derives much support from other passages of Holy Writ. Thus Christ is constantly spoken of in Romans v., as the One Whose obedience makes many righteous. His Crucifixion is repeatedly referred to as the Crucifixion of all who believe in Him,[3] while in the Epistle to the Hebrews He is said to have "tasted death for every man." [4] Another class of passages is contained in the Epistle to the Hebrews. There the great High Priest is represented as entering into heaven, the true Holy of Holies, to offer and plead the Sacrifice once offered for the sins of the whole world.[5] And here I may stop to notice a misconception into which theologians of repute have fallen. In the Hebrew ritual the victim was not slain, as is often said, *upon* the altar. It was slain "before the Lord," [6] and *after its death* was solemnly pre-

---

[1] 2 Cor. v. 14.   [2] Note 20.
[3] Rom. vi. 6. Cp. Gal. ii. 20, vi. 14, 17.   [4] Heb. ii. 9.
[5] Heb. iv. 14, vii. 26, 27, viii. 3–6, ix. 12, 24, &c.
[6] Exod. xxix. 11, 16, 20, 25; Lev. i. 3, 5 (where observe the words "*bring* the blood"), 11, 16, iii. 2, 8, iv. 4, 15, 24, 29, vi. 25, vii. 2, viii. 19–21, 28, &c. In Exod. xx. 24 we have a command to *sacrifice* (זבח) the victim *on the altar*. Yet though the original meaning of זבח is to slay, it afterwards came to be the technical word for offering in sacrifice. When Moses wishes to speak of the act of slaying he uses the word שחט. When he speaks of performing all the ceremonial rites he uses the term עשה. See Exod. xxix. 41.

sented to God, either by being burned entire upon the altar,[1] or by the consumption of a portion of it upon the altar by fire,[2] and the sprinkling of its blood upon the veil of the sanctuary and upon the horns of the altar of incense,[3] or by sprinkling the blood upon and pouring it beside the altar of burnt sacrifice,[4] or, as on the great Day of Atonement, by sprinkling it upon the mercy-seat.[5] Thus is typified Christ, our great High Priest, Who *after* having given up His life for our sakes, enters for ever into heaven to present that Life, so eternally well-pleasing unto His heavenly Father, as a perpetual Propitiatory Sacrifice for all our misdoings. Once given up upon the Cross, that Life, that Unspotted Humanity, is for ever presenting Itself before God in the Holy Place of the heavens; that Lamb as it had been slain is ever before the Father of all; that Blood lies sprinkled upon the true mercy-seat of the Divine Love for evermore.

Another class of texts is frequently overlooked; so much so that they may be said to form no part whatever of the theology of the Passion as it is taught by most divines of the present age. I refer to those striking passages which speak of the unifying effects of the Saviour's Death. While it is continually regarded as a means of offering that which the Mosaic Law ever taught to be the principle of life, it also is spoken of as removing not only all barriers between God and man, but between man and his fellow. Not only were the decrees of condemnation issued by a Just God against unrighteous man taken out of the way by being affixed to the Cross of Christ; not only was that

---

[1] Lev. i. 9. 17.
[2] Lev. iii. 3, 9, 14, iv. 9, 10, 26, 31, v. 10, vii. 3–5, &c.
[3] Lev. iv. 6, 7, 17, 18.   [4] Lev. iv. 34, vii. 2, 5.   [5] Lev. xvi. 14.

Death of the Lord Jesus a most emphatic condemnation of sin; but it placed all mankind from henceforth on a common ground; it removed for ever the distinction between Jew and Gentile. Henceforth all were God's covenant people. All were alike reconciled in the Person of Jesus Christ to the Father. No law of commandments formulated in decrees[1] could henceforth stand between man and God, since He, in His flesh, had fulfilled them all. And so henceforth Jew and Gentile were one in Him. The middle wall of partition was broken down by Christ upon the Cross, and from henceforth all men alike had access by One Spirit unto the Father.

We meet again, especially in the writings of St. John and in the Epistle to the Hebrews, allusions to the *cleansing* effects of the Blood of Christ.[2] But we cannot be satisfied with any explanation which confines this cleansing to the forensic sense of mere acquittal. However true it may be that in the initial stage of the work of salvation God accepts us by virtue of our union with His Beloved Son as being what apart from Him we are not and cannot be, namely, free from guilt, it is none the less true that this purifying, cleansing, sanctifying effect of Christ's Blood is a *real* process; that faith in the Life, the obedience, the Sacrifice of Christ tends to bring about conformity to its spirit, that he who has such a faith becomes *saturated*, if we may so speak, with that spirit of obedience and sacrifice which is manifested in the life of Christ, that he learns to hate sin as Jesus hates it, to condemn it as He condemns it, that sin thus ceases to have dominion

---

[1] τὸν νόμον τῶν ἐντολῶν ἐν δόγμασιν.
[2] Heb. i. 3, ix. 14; 1 John i. 7, 9; Rev. i. 5, vii. 14. See also 1 Cor. vi. 11.

over him, that the condemnation of the law loses its power, that the law itself is no more needed, because the fulness of an indwelling Spirit translates him from a condition of bondage into the abiding favour of a gracious God.

Once more, we have passages which refer to Christ as our ἱλασμός, our ἱλαστήριον.[1] There can be no question that they point to Christ as One Who rendered God favourable to man; that His coming, His Work on earth, produced a change in the relations between the two. The former term points Christ out to us as the actual propitiating force itself. It identifies Christ's Person and His Work. The latter represents Him as the meeting-point between God and man; the true Mercy-Seat with the Divine Shekinah resting upon it, as well as the Blood of the Sacrificed Victim once shed for sin, but now presented in the Presence of God throughout the ages. *How* God is propitiated we are not informed. That by the Person and Work of Christ He *is* propitiated we are distinctly told.

But in two passages of Scripture the plan of redemption is yet further unfolded. I speak of the 53rd chapter of Isaiah and its paraphrase in the 1st Epistle of St Peter.[2] There we are told that Christ bare our sins in His own Body on the tree; that the chastisement of our peace was upon Him, that by His stripes we are healed, and in stronger language still, that the Lord hath laid on Him the iniquity of us all. There can be no doubt that such language as this is susceptible of the common interpretation, namely, that Christ bore the punishment that we had deserved, and that the justice of God was satisfied thereby. It is a reasonable and therefore a permissible explana-

---

[1] Note 21. [2] Chap. ii. 21–24.

tion of the language. All I would contend is, that it is not the only permissible interpretation. The Prophet does not formulate in definite language the doctrine that by laying our iniquity on Christ, God's justice was satisfied, and man thereby freed from liability to punishment. That there was a moral necessity that Christ, in order to raise man from his lost and fallen condition, should Himself descend into it; that in working out our restoration the burden and weight of our sins should fall on His shoulders, that it should be "laid on Him," or by a translation equally admissible should "lay hold on Him," is intelligible enough. But it does not therefore follow that the whole process of atonement is properly explained by representing this sorrow and suffering as satisfying God's justice and so securing our immunity from punishment.[1]

One more passage remains to be noticed, because we shall see hereafter that it formed the foundation of the system of a divine of our own University to whose originality and power sufficient justice has not, I think, been done. It is the verse in the Epistle to the Romans which speaks of our old man being crucified with Christ, in order that the body of sin might be destroyed.[2] Whether this is a Hebraism for sinful body or not, and whether the passage means that our present human body, called elsewhere by the Apostle a body of death, must first suffer dissolution that by Christ's power we may inherit a new body more fitted for our high calling as Christians, or whether it does not, we cannot say. But the passage is a remarkable one, and has not yet received the attention it deserves.

It remains to endeavour to clear up a few misconcep-

[1] Note 22.   [2] Rom. vi. 6–8.

tions, which, though they may have little influence over theologians, have an immense influence over the popular mind in its interpretation of the Bible. The chief of these are the ideas popularly imported into the words Mediator, Atonement, Remission. The Mediatorial office of Christ is frequently represented as entirely confined to His suffering and dying upon the Cross for our sins. As a matter of fact it embraces everything that He can be said to have done for us, or to be doing for us now. The word "Mediator" signifies simply a go-between; one who acts with one person on behalf of another. The Mediation of Christ includes His spotless life of love and mercy, His conquest over sin and death, His carrying our human nature into the Presence of God, His re-creation of us in the Divine Image by the agency of His Spirit, just as much as His Sufferings and Death. Yet so rooted is the conception in people's minds that mediation means substitution to bear our punishment, that I have known many to have entirely misconceived the whole argument of Bishop Butler on this subject in his *Analogy* simply and solely because he uses the word mediation in its legitimate and natural sense.

The word Atonement, again, which is used in our translation of the New Testament as equivalent to reconciliation, has come in the popular mouth to mean satisfaction to God by bearing the punishment of death for our sins. The preaching of the Atonement is no longer, as it was of old, the simple proclamation of the fact that God and man are one. It means preaching that Christ by His death upon the Cross bore the punishment of our sins, and so satisfied the justice of the Father, and won pardon for us. Yet the word At-one-ment simply means the making one, without any reference to the process by which that union is accomplished. And in the Old Testament the word atonement is used as the translation of the word *caphar*, which is equivalent to our *cover*, and means to conceal, to hide from sight. That it is in every instance but one used in connection with sacrifice in the Old Testament is unquestionably the fact. But what is contended is, that while sacrifice has the effect of hiding, concealing, doing away our sins, has in fact the effect of making us one with God, it is nowhere even intimated that this takes place by the substitution of a victim to bear the punishment of the offender. In the New Testament the word Atonement only occurs once, and there it occurs as the translation of a word elsewhere rendered "reconciliation," a word which is not in the slightest degree sacrificial in its character.

The same may be said of the word remission. Bishop Pearson, in a careful note on the tenth Article of the Creed, has pointed out five senses in which the word ἀφιέναι is used in Scripture. It may not unreasonably be asked what right we have, when dealing with a process so complex as the restoration of mankind through Jesus Christ, to select the one idea of *forgiveness* as represented by the word ἄφεσις and leave all the others out of sight.

One more observation may be permitted. The idea of Propitiation is sometimes imported into passages which were intended to have a wider range. Thus the text " God so loved the world that He gave His only-begotten Son, to the end that all that believe in Him should not perish, but have everlasting life," is interpreted " God gave His Son to die upon the Cross, to the end that all that believe in the saving efficacy of that Death should have everlasting Life." I believe it would not be too much to affirm that this interpretation of the passage was unknown for the first 1500 years of the Church's history. Christ was given, not simply to make satisfaction for our sins, but to impart to us the Life that is in Him. Thus He says He will "give His Flesh for the life of the world." In what way He will give it, He explains immediately. His Flesh is to be the Bread, that is the staff and support of our life. We are to eat It, and to drink His Blood. That is to say, by a mystical and spiritual process, of which faith is an essential element, the Flesh of the Paschal Lamb, the Very Humanity of the Incarnate Lord, is to pass into us and become ours. Thus we once more find ourselves in the presence of the fact that the central doctrine of the Christian faith is not belief in the fact of a reconciliation once made in times past between us and God by the Sacrifice on the Cross, but in the restoration in us of the lost Image of God by the Divine Spirit through the Incarnation, the Perfect Obedience, the Exaltation, of Jesus Christ.

To sum up what has been said. We have inquired into the origin of sacrifice, and we have found that though a good deal more may reasonably be deduced from it, no more is necessarily involved in it than a feeling of gratitude, prompting us to surrender absolutely to God whatever is of most value in our sight, as an acknowledgment of all we owe to Him, a public and practical expression of the feelings of the human heart. We have examined the Sacrifices of the old Law, and we find them based upon a principle already recognized by the progenitors of the Jewish people, but we find no proof that the practice of animal sacrifice originated in the direct command of God. Neither in the Ritual of the Law, nor in the expressions which it uses in reference to the effect of the sacrifices, do we detect any direct assertion of the principle of substitution. This principle may take its place among many rational and tenable explanations or illustrations of the Mosaic ceremonial, but it is no more than a mode of elucidation of the truth—it cannot claim to be either directly affirmed, or necessarily gathered from the plain declarations of Holy Writ.

The utterances of the writers of the New Testament concerning the effects of Christ's Death next came under review. We have found that they represent the Lord's Death not in one, but in various aspects. It is a price paid for us and for our sins. It is the bearing of a curse which lay upon us.[1] It is a Representative Death of Humanity. It is a slaying of a body of sin. It is the great unifying principle of the world. It not only procures our acquittal, but it imparts holiness. It not only removes the guilt of sin, but it removes sin itself. And among all these statements there is not one single passage which explicitly asserts that it derived its reconciling power from its being the bearing the Divine wrath for sin in our stead. This may or may not be a necessary deduction from the repeated declaration that Christ's Blood was the price paid for our sins, and that He was made "a curse," and "sin" for us. But it is an inference from the language of Scripture, let us bear in mind, not the express language of Scripture itself. It may be a legitimate and

---

[1] Not necessarily that God's wrath or justice was satisfied by laying the curse on His Son, but because His willingness to bear it at once manifested Divine Love and human perfection.

necessary inference, or it may not. If it be, its necessity must be rigidly demonstrated. And unless it be so demonstrated, we can have no right to impugn the orthodoxy of those who resort to other explanations of the Lord's Propitiatory work, in order to avoid the very serious difficulties which beset this theory, when it is propounded for our acceptance, not as a possible explanation, or contribution toward the explanation, of a stupendous mystery, but as a fundamental article of faith. On the other hand, we have every right to protest against the unfairness of those who, in the face of the fact which I trust to be able to establish in my next lecture, that the vast majority of Christian thinkers have rejected, and do still reject, this explanation,—persist in representing it to mankind as the cardinal principle upon which Christianity depends.[1]

[1] Note 23.

LECTURE III.

THEORIES OF PROPITIATION IN THE CHRISTIAN CHURCH.

"We know in part, and we prophesy in part. But when that which is perfect is come, then that which is in part shall be done away."—
1 COR. xiii. 9, 10.

WE have now examined the teaching of Holy Scripture on the subject of propitiation for sin. Our next step is to ascertain what explanation the statements of Scripture have received among theologians of various ages and schools. And here we shall find that instead of one uniform statement of doctrine, the utmost variety of interpretation has been placed upon the language of Scripture. It is no less strange than true, that in spite of the almost irresistible tendency of early theology to formulate theological propositions, the doctrine of Propitiation was never touched by it. No Oecumenical Council was ever assembled to decide on the way in which Christ's offering of Himself availed to put away our sins. No early Father attempted to dogmatize on the subject. It was reserved for Protestant theology to make the Death of Christ rather than

His Incarnation the key-stone of the Gospel system, and to make the acceptance of a particular theory respecting that Death, not only the *articulus stantis aut cadentis ecclesiæ*, but the indispensable requisite for the salvation of the individual soul.

The earliest writers of the Christian Church kept strictly within the limits of the language of the New Testament. Clement of Rome, the earliest of these writers, insists only upon the preciousness of Christ's Blood in the Father's sight, seeing that that Blood when shed had virtue enough to effect the salvation of the whole world.[1] The writing which was put forth in the name of the Apostle Barnabas contents itself with saying that were it not for our sakes, it were impossible that Christ could have suffered.[2] Ignatius calls faith Christ's Flesh and love His Blood, and again speaks of the Blood of Christ as "incorruptible love and eternal life."[3] Justin Martyr, in his somewhat voluminous discourses, makes but little reference to Christ's Death. And when he does refer to it, he takes care to deny that Jesus was cursed by God, although he grants that Jesus took on Him the curse of all men, and suffered on behalf of the whole family of mankind. His theory of redemption, as it is laid down in a fragment of his writings which has been accidentally preserved, is that the only way in which human corruption could be removed was by destroying its cause (or more literally its corruption-making essence), and that this could be done in no other way than by uniting true life with that which had become corrupted, and by this union delivering the latter from the disease which had infected it. Thus it is to the

[1] Note 1.   [2] Note 2.
[3] Note 3.

taking of our nature by Jesus Christ, and not to His Death upon the Cross, that our deliverance from sin is attributed.[1]

Irenæus is the first writer who deliberately formulates a theory on the subject of redemption. But in the assertion of this theory he is by no means consistent. He is very anxious, in answer to the Gnostics, to provide those for whom he is writing with a *rationale* of their belief. But it is quite clear from his other utterances that he does not consider his explanation an exhaustive or a binding one. He argues that God was too fair, even to Satan, to redeem mankind from his power by force. He therefore caused an adequate price to be paid for this redemption, and this price was the Death and sufferings of Christ.[2] The great thinker and divine, Origen, seems to have included this notion in his teaching concerning the Death of Christ, rather than to have put it forward as the entire explanation of that death.[3] In the succeeding century the idea seems to have taken deeper root. Gregory of Nyssa embraced it,[4] Augustin propounded it in a true legal form when he taught that Satan lost his right to enslave mankind by allowing his hatred to them to carry him so far as to slay One Who had never committed sin. He even contended that it would have been unjust of God to deprive Satan of his empire over the souls of men, unless an adequate equivalent were paid to him.[5] And if a difficulty presented itself as to how Satan was induced to accept this equivalent, and so lose his power over men, the answer was also ready. Satan was deceived, or rather, he deceived himself. In his bitter hatred to all mankind, he

---

[1] Note 4.   [2] Note 5.   [3] Note 6.
[4] Note 7.   [5] Note 8.

wreaked his vengeance upon the only One Whom he had not been able to lead astray, and then found, to his surprise, that by exacting the penalty of sin from One Who had not deserved to incur it, he had forfeited his power over the whole human race.[1] The commanding influence of Augustin ensured the reception of this doctrine in the West. In the East its acceptance was less general. Not only, as has been said, was no attempt made to lay down authoritatively the conditions which made the Sacrifice of Christ a Propitiation for sin, but many of the Fathers explicitly or implicitly rejected the explanation which has been mentioned. Irenaeus himself, the author of that explanation, provides his readers with an alternative theory. The disobedience of man which had taken place by means of a tree was set right by the obedience displayed on the tree of Calvary; and it is by this obedience unto death that man is reconciled to God. Athanasius never swerves from the theory he lays down in his early treatise on the Incarnation. Jesus died, he teaches, in order that, on the one hand He may do so in the place of[2] all, and on the other, being Himself immortal through the union of the Godhead and the Manhood, He might preserve His own Body from corruption, and raise it to eternal life, and might thus impart the immortality He Himself possessed to all for whom he died.[3]

Gregory of Nazianzus, who rose to the primacy of the Churches in the East, distinctly denies that the price paid by Jesus Christ for our redemption was paid either to the Devil or to God. How, he emphatically asks, can God Himself be the ransom paid to the evil one? And how could the price be paid to God, Who did not hold us

[1] Note 9.   [2] ἀντί.   [3] Note 10.

captive? It was sufficient, he declared, to believe that by God's dispensation Christ was appointed to die, that not this man merely, nor that, but that the whole human race should be brought back to God.[1] His famous successor in the chair of Constantinople, the illustrious orator of the Christian Church, St. John Chrysostom, when dealing with a crucial passage such as that which declares that Christ was made sin for us, says no more than this, that Christ, by enduring not only to die for us, but to die as one cursed, thereby freely bestowed upon us blessings beyond everything we looked for, so that we should fear these words more than hell, and deem it grievous, not to be punished, but to sin. Again, in dealing with another crucial passage, Gal. iii. 13, which speaks of Christ as being "made a curse for us," he expounds it thus: Since he who hangs on a tree is cursed, and he who transgresses the law is accursed, it was not necessary that He Who was about to destroy this last curse should Himself undergo it, but rather that He should submit to the endurance of another curse instead of it. This He did, and by enduring the latter curse He destroyed the former. And just as, when a man is condemned to death, another man who is not liable to that fate removes from him the punishment by electing to bear it himself, this is what Christ did. For though not liable to the curse which is affixed to transgression, Christ accepted the curse of death in its stead, that He might destroy the curse under which men lay.[2] In other words, Christ bore one kind of curse, that He might remove another from us.[3]

Another great Divine of the ancient Church, Cyril of Alexandria, says but little upon the passages on which

---

[1] Note 11.   [2] *i.e.* the curse of transgression.   [3] Note 12.

modern Protestant theology lays such great stress, but declares once more that Christ suffered according to the dispensation of God; and this in order that He might trample death under foot; and then, because He was life, and the Giver of life, He might transelement our body, which had been made subject to the tyranny of death, into the incorruption in which He Himself for ever dwelt. Christ's death, he adds elsewhere, was an exchange for our life, His righteousness accepted in the place of ours.[1]

It is clear that many of these early writers, whose attention was taken up with the true theory of the Incarnation of Christ, had not dwelt much upon the difficulties and mysteries connected with His Death. Some had jumped to a hasty and unsatisfactory conclusion on the subject, and others had given it scarcely any consideration at all. And so things remained till the days of that famous Saint and Archbishop of our own church, Anselm, on whose mind the difficulty pressed so much that he wrote a treatise to clear it up. And here we find ourselves for the first time face to face with that doctrine which in later times has become so nearly universal in the Reformed Churches, the idea, namely, that God became man, not in order to reunite man to God, but in order that adequate satisfaction should be made to the dignity of God, outraged by sin. Anselm's theory, briefly stated, is as follows. Sin is the neglecting to pay God the honour due to Him. Punishment is the exacting of satisfaction by Him for this neglect. God cannot as the Righteous Governor of the world suffer sin to go unpunished. Therefore for every sin, either satisfaction must be made or punishment exacted. Man cannot make sufficient satisfaction to God

[1] Note 13.

for sin. Only a Divine Being could do this. But as man has sinned man must make satisfaction for sin. Hence the reason that God becomes man, that man may make to God the satisfaction he otherwise could not have made. To vindicate God's honour, the sinless Son of God must die. And for that Sacrifice He can claim a reward. But since He to whom all belongs can receive no reward, it were only meet to give the reward He has earned to those for whom He suffered.[1] The rationalizing Abelard, who anticipated so many of our nineteenth century speculations, rejects this theory, and instead propounds one familiar to us of late, that God's love to man, displayed in the giving up of His Son to Death for us, was so amazing an example of Divine compassion, that it must needs move us to a corresponding affection. It would be unprofitable were we to do more than take a glance at the theories of the Schoolmen. Alexander de Hales appears to have been the first who held the theory of an equivalent, so popular since his time. Aquinas, the greatest of the mediæval doctors, rejected the notion that there was any necessity in the nature of things that Christ should suffer for us, but if He suffered, it was in order that God might thereby manifest the love He had to all mankind. His doctrine of satisfaction is very striking. The Death of Christ satisfied the requirements of God, because it gave Him something He loved as much as, or more than, He hated sin. And thus it was that the Sacrifice of Christ, well pleasing as it was in the eyes of God, had power to redeem us from sin.[2]

The Reformation gave a new turn to speculation on this head. In fact, the doctrine of Atonement by the Blood of Christ became, in the eyes of the members of the

[1] Note 14.   [2] Note 15.

Reformed Communions, what the Incarnation had been in the view of earlier times, the central doctrine of the Christian faith. Martin Luther made his whole system depend upon the interchange brought about by faith between Christ and ourselves. Christ became all we deserved to be, and thus by faith we became all that He is. We deserved to be accursed of God for sin. He bore that curse for us, and thus we were freed from it. By His Death on the Cross our sins became His. By faith in that Death His Righteousness became ours. His Righteousness, it is true, did not cease to be His, as our sins ceased to be ours, because that righteousness was not overcome by our sins, but overcame them—utterly consumed and burned them up. But from the time that we believed that Jesus died and rose again, there was so close and constant an union and conjunction between Christ and us, that His Righteousness for ever sprung and bubbled up within us, even as He said, "The water which I will give you shall be in you a well of water, springing up unto everlasting life." Calvin's view is characteristically different. Luther's impulsive grasp of revealed truth is lacking in logical form. Calvin is less penetrated with the sense of God's loving-kindness, but his keen logical intellect sees difficulties where Luther sees none. "God was not, could not be," says Calvin, "hostile to, or angry with 'His Beloved Son, in whom He was well pleased.' Yet nevertheless He suffered the weight of Divine severity, since, smitten and afflicted by the Hand of God, He experienced all the signs of an angry and a punishing Deity."[1]

The Confessions of the Reformed Churches differ a good

[1] Note 16.

deal in their treatment of this question. Some go into detail, and some do not. The Saxon Confession, drawn up by Melanchthon, is interesting as expressing the views of that Reformer. In it we find the assertion that "no reconciliation can be made unless punishment be fully endured. Such is the greatness of God's anger, that the Eternal Father could not be appeased, but by the intercession and Death of the Son." But our chief attention will be given to those Confessions which have not merely an historical or archæological interest, but have maintained their position to the present day. And here on the one hand we have our own Thirty-nine Articles, the Augsburg Confession, still accepted by the Lutheran bodies, and the Helvetic Confession, still recognized by the Swiss Reformed communion, and on the other the Belgic Confession, and the decrees of the Synod of Dort, which are the standards of the Dutch Reformed communion, and the Westminster Confession, which, as well as the Larger and Shorter Catechisms, are the standards of faith in the Presbyterian bodies of Scotland. The Augsburg Confession uses language identical with that of the Thirty-nine Articles. It declares no more than this, that Christ truly suffered, was crucified, died and was buried to reconcile us to the Father, and that He was a sacrifice, not only for original guilt, but for all actual sins of men. The Helvetic Confession confines itself to the statement that Christ, by His Passion and Death, reconciled the heavenly Father to all the faithful, expiated sin, brought death to nought, and destroyed hell and damnation. The Belgic Confession, on the other hand, lays it down not only that our Lord assumed the nature which had sinned through disobedience, and that in that very nature He made satisfaction, but that He, by His bitter Death and Passion, bore the just penalties of sin. The Synod of Dort, in decrees which still form part of the doctrinal standards of the Dutch Reformed Church, formulates the doctrine thus: that Jesus Christ, in order to make satisfaction for us, was made on the Cross sin and a curse for us, or in our stead. The Westminster Confession, which is accepted by the Presbyterian communions in Scotland, states the matter in this way: "The Lord Jesus, by His perfect obedience and sacrifice of Himself, which He through the Eternal Spirit once offered up unto God, hath fully satisfied the justice of His Father, and purchased not only reconciliation, but an everlasting inheritance in the kingdom of heaven for all those whom the Father hath given to Him." Here the satisfaction to the Father is not attributed to the sufferings of the Saviour, but to His "obedience and sacrifice." The Catechisms, however, do not confine themselves to this statement. The Larger Catechism, intended for more advanced Christians, declares that "it was requisite that the Mediator should be God, that He might sustain and keep the human nature from sinking under the infinite wrath of God, and the power of death, give worth and efficacy to His sufferings, obedience and intercession, and to satisfy God's justice, procure His favour, purchase a peculiar people, give His Spirit unto them, conquer all their enemies and bring them to everlasting salvation."[1] While the Shorter and simpler Catechism explains that Christ "executeth the office of a Priest in His once offering up Himself a sacrifice to satisfy Divine Justice and reconcile us to God."[2] What the accepted

---

[1] Larger Catechism, Q. 38.
[2] Shorter Catechism, Q. 25. See Note 17.

doctrine of the Calvinistic bodies was on this subject we have already seen in our first lecture. It taught that Jesus Christ made satisfaction for our sins by bearing, either the wrath of the Father which was due to us, as some think, or an equivalent to that wrath, as others taught. Jonathan Edwards, as we have seen, stands alone, by reason of his pre-eminent logical acuteness, in denying that Jesus Christ suffered either, and in asserting that what He did bear was a clear and full apprehension of the true nature of sin, which, though he evidently feels that it were equivalent to the punishment we deserved, he still shrinks from affirming to be such an equivalent. He differs from other Calvinist divines, moreover, in asserting that it was Christ's obedience rather than His sufferings, which made satisfaction to the Father. Others, however, have gone so far as to say that Christ must suffer an equivalent to the torments of hell, to satisfy the Father's wrath. Endure them in duration He could not, being God's Well-beloved Son; but there was in Him, being God as well as man, such an infinite capacity for suffering, that He could endure in one moment agonies equivalent to what in us would require an eternity of torment to exhaust. This tremendous doctrine has been recently revived by a Lutheran Divine, but it does not seem to have been generally accepted. But the universal doctrine of the earlier Calvinists was that God required a satisfaction of His justice, which satisfaction was given, as some taught by the obedience, as others supposed, by the sufferings of Christ. The doctrine of the Arminian Grotius, however, has been revived by a later Calvinistic school. This doctrine taught that the necessity for an Atonement arose from the fact of God's moral government of the world. He needed no personal satisfaction to His outraged honour on the part of the offender or his representative. But were He to pass over sin by simply forgiving it, He would encourage men to sin, and thus destroy the foundations of human morality. This school also protested against the limitation of the Atonement which was an article of faith with Calvin and his immediate followers. Owen puts the matter thus in his assertion that Christ did not die for all, but only for the elect: "Either Christ underwent the pains of hell," he says, "for all the sins of all men, in which case all must be saved; or some sins of all men, in which case no man can be saved, or all the sins of some men, in which case the elect and they only can be saved."[1] This keen and incisive logic was perceived to contain a fallacy which could better be felt than answered, and accordingly the later school of Calvinism sheltered itself behind the plain declaration of Scripture, that Christ died for all. Still, the notion of a substitution of Christ in some sense for ourselves, as bearing the punishment due to sin, continued to be a prominent feature in their teaching.

For nearly three centuries this theory, that Christ made satisfaction to the Father by bearing as our substitute God's wrath against sin, has been the accepted doctrine of the Reformed communions, though not, as we have seen, formally required by the standards of each particular body. The Church of Rome has consistently refused her sanction to this view of Atonement. Neither in the decrees nor the Catechism of the Council of Trent does any such doctrine find a place. On this point the language of the Church of Rome is singularly cautious and Scriptural.

[1] Note 18.

"Jesus Christ merited justification," we are told, "for us, by His most holy Passion on the wood of the Cross, and for us made satisfaction unto God the Father." And well and wisely does the Catechism of the Council of Trent speak of the "Mystery of the Cross" as "far beyond human reason." This caution has extended even to our own time. In one of those friendly discussions which form so pleasing a feature in our modern theological controversy, one of the Bishops of the Roman Church, at the request of Cardinal Manning, communicates to a periodical of the day the following statement of the doctrine of his Communion. Following Aquinas he ascribes the virtues of the Atonement to the fact that the "retributive act" of Christ is more pleasing to God than the act to be atoned for was displeasing. "We had sinned," he continues. "We had incurred the sentence of death. Christ therefore must die for us—the just for the unjust." Beyond this careful and truly Scriptural statement the Bishop makes no demand whatever upon our faith, offers no explanation whatever concerning this amazing mystery. Would that all Protestant theologians had so felt; and would that the Church of Rome had been as cautious and Scriptural on other points as she has been on this![1]

The history of the doctrine would not, however, be complete without a mention of one remarkable and most original protest against the received doctrine in the last century. That profound and thoughtful divine, William Law, in a defence of revealed religion which he issued in 1739, lays down a view of the effects of Christ's Death which is absolutely unique. He protests against the notion that God could be angry in His own essential

[1] Note 19.

nature, "Who is only infinite, unalterable, overflowing Love." God's wrath against sin was nothing more than a "plague or evil that sin had brought forth in Nature." It was such a wrath as "God Himself hates, just as He hates sin," and which He burns to destroy. He felt no anger against fallen man, but only a Divine pity and love. Seeing that nothing less could bring the miserable state of things to an end, He sent His Only Begotten Son into the world to bring to an end the eternal wrath of Death and Hell. Now if Adam were to be the father of a race that could become sons of God, it was necessary that this state of things should cease. But what was the state of things? Man's original life was corrupted and destroyed. His earthly and fleshly life was only one common to him and the beasts. That life must be destroyed, its blood poured out, its whole existence annihilated, before the children of Adam could become the children of God. The divine life which was breathed into him when man became a living soul must be rekindled or regenerated. Human nature must put off all it had put on, and put on all that it had put off. Therefore Christ took upon Him our sinful flesh. He condemned and destroyed sin in the flesh by overcoming temptation; He destroyed the animal life to which mankind had been reduced by sacrificing it upon the Cross. Thus He destroyed both the first and second death which stood between us and our possession once more of the Image of God. As man had lost Paradise, and become liable to death, so Christ reversing the process endured death and restored us to Paradise.[1]

No theologian has embraced or even taken the least notice of this remarkable theory. But in the present

[1] Note 20.

century there has been a decided reaction against what had become the accepted doctrine of the Reformed Churches. To say nothing of Schleiermacher's ingenious theory that Christ's active obedience was a satisfaction for sin, but was not vicarious, and that His passive obedience was vicarious, and was not a satisfaction for sin;[1] nor of Edward Irving's emphatic condemnation of what he stigmatized as the "bargain and barter hypothesis,"[2] there are four main channels in which that modern theological thought which rejects the substitution theory has flowed. The first is that of Abelard, revived in modern times by Bushnell and others, which regards the Sacrifice as a manifestation of Divine Love, moving men to repay love by love, and so winning them back to God. The second is that which represents Christ as our example, pointing out to us in His sufferings and Death what is the true life of humanity, and how we all must rise to righteousness by following in the steps of our suffering and dying Master.[3] The third is that which supposes that Christ, in dying for our sins, was obeying and fulfilling to the uttermost the law of our being; that to redeem us from sin— they are the very words, we may remark by the way, of Cyril of Alexandria—He must "enter into the lowest condition into which we had fallen by sin;" that He must offer to God as the representative of us all "an entire surrender of the whole Spirit and body to God," and that this is to "reconcile God to man."[4] The fourth is that which is explained at length in the very remarkable treatise of the late Dr. McLeod Campbell, and it is followed and stated with far greater clearness by the well-known theologian and expositor, Godet. Dr. McLeod Campbell's

[1] Note 21.   [2] Note 22.   [3] Note 23.   [4] Note 24.

theory divides the work of Christ in making propitiation for sin (atonement, as he wrongly calls it, whereas it is no more than a step towards the Atonement) into two parts, a retrospective and a prospective action on our behalf. Each of these may be regarded in two points of view, as a dealing with men on behalf of God, and a dealing with God on the part of men. The way in which Jesus Christ witnessed for God to men in reference to the past was by becoming a "living epistle of the grace of God." He manifested the Divine perfection, He displayed God's hatred of sin, and love to all mankind; His sorrows were the manifestation of God's eternal hatred of sin; His whole life was such a revelation of the Father's attitude to sin and to mankind, that He could truly say to His disciples, "He that hath seen Me hath seen the Father." On the other hand, He acted on behalf of man toward God by displaying on man's part the attitude which man ought to assume towards sin and towards God. His hatred to sin as man was identical with God's hatred to sin. He presented on behalf of all mankind as their representative a full and sufficient acknowledgment of their guilt; a full and sufficient repentance for having committed it. His sorrows were no penal infliction of God's wrath, but the simple result of His full realization of the position in which those for whom He pleaded, and with whom He was identified, had placed themselves by their transgression. His death was "the Amen of Humanity" to the just and righteous sentence, "the wages of sin is death." Again, the aspect of the Atonement, as it regarded the future, was to display God as having opened the pathway to reconciliation to man through the Blood of His Son, and as yearning to receive all mankind back on the footing of that reconciliation; and to enable man to understand how the handwriting of his sins was for ever blotted out, and that henceforth through Christ's obedience and reconciling work peace and joy, and an entire confidence in God's love and favour, could take the place of that sense of guilt and separation from God which must weigh on him until he could feel that an Atonement had been made. Godet expresses similar ideas in somewhat different language. He divides Christ's work into two parts, Christ's work *for* us, and Christ's work *in* us. The former depends upon God's Eternal hatred of evil, which is a necessary part of His being. That hatred is felt by Him to every man so far as he is tending to become evil, and is consolidated into actual hatred when the man becomes wholly evil. But by Christ's work this condition of things may be avoided. He came first to remove the results of the Fall, and next to re-establish in us that sanctity which we had lost. A sinless one must perish that it may be clear that he perishes not for his own sins, but for the recognition of the principle that mankind had deserved death for their rebellion against God. Next, it is necessary that He Who comes to repair the evil of the Fall, must concur with a holy energy in God's repairing work. In Jesus Christ we have the true ἱλαστήριον, the mercy-seat where God's holiness and man's sinfulness meet. He alone can make propitiation for sin. For while He stands in the form and as the representative of sinners, He hates sin as God hates it, He condemns it, as only a being of perfect holiness can condemn it. We obtain part in that redemption by faith, but this faith is no mere *opus operatum*. We must concur with all our heart and soul in the redeeming work. We must be associated with Jesus Christ in His task on behalf of humanity. We must admit that we deserved the sentence of death which He accepted on our behalf. Christ's work in us is the result of this faith, producing in us an initial condition of reconcilement to God which enables us to apply the work of Christ to our souls without any uncertainty as to the way in which God regards us; and then going on to impart to us the actual mind and spirit of Christ as regards sin and as regards holiness. "Jesus," he concludes, "is necessary to the human soul because He has become our indispensable fellow-worker in the accomplishment of its supreme endeavour; the realization of its moral destination." [1]

Such, my brethren, is as full a sketch as is permitted by the limits to which I am confined, of the various theories regarding Christ's redemptive work which have been held and taught in the Church of God. They are sufficient to show, that while the fact that Christ's death was a Propitiatory Sacrifice for sin, has been generally, if not universally, recognized by those who call themselves Christians, the explanations given of the fact have been most various. In the early Church the writers concerning Christ's redemptive work may be divided into two classes, those who explained it wrongly, and those who did not explain it at all. Are we bound to believe that those who have more recently taken upon themselves to explain it have been more successful? to accept their teaching when, without any claim to infallibility such as is put forward by the Church of Rome, they nevertheless demand that we shall receive as a condition of salvation the theory that our salvation has been effected by Christ bearing the Father's wrath against sin as our substitute,

[1] Note 25.

and that we are justified and saved solely by the imputation of His merits to us through faith? We have seen that some of the clearest thinkers of this school have been conscious of the difficulties of the theory; that they have admitted that it was impossible that the Beloved Son of God could be conscious of being the object of His wrath; that they have substituted Christ's obedience for His bearing the Father's wrath as the efficient cause of the satisfaction He made for sin, and that many have intermingled the idea of Christ's obedience with that of His bearing the Father's wrath as constituting the essence of that satisfaction. Thus, then, the popular theory that Christ made atonement for our sins by bearing the Father's wrath against sin in our stead, is not only without the slightest support from the Church before the Reformation, but is rejected by some theologians of the greatest note after that period. It forms no part of the theological standards of our own or the Lutheran Churches. It is repudiated by Calvin; it is expressly rejected by Jonathan Edwards. And it is qualified among other Protestant theologians of repute by being associated with Christ's obedience as the ground of His satisfaction for sin. And thus it would seem abundantly clear that in rejecting this form of the doctrine of satisfaction, a man is not necessarily rejecting the Christian scheme. And not only so, but there is another serious objection interposed by Church History in the way of our acceptance of this theory as the only true explanation of the mystery of Christ's Death. This objection consists in the fact that for fifteen centuries the main reason of Christ's Incarnation was held to be, not that He should simply make satisfaction for sin, but that He should remove it; that He should restore mankind to the condition of holiness and incorruption which they had lost. Satisfaction for sin was no doubt a necessary step in the task, since sin existed, and had to be put away. But Christ became human, so Scripture and Catholic antiquity witness with one voice, that man might become divine. He did not come to carry out a scheme whereby men might be considered and treated as if they were holy, He came that they might become so in very truth. He came, not merely to enable us to escape the effects of sin, but to "put away sin by the Sacrifice of Himself." That the first effect of His redeeming work on the reconciled soul will be to destroy all fear of punishment and sense of alienation is not denied; but what is asserted is, that this blessed sense of reconciliation must lead, by a natural and not an arbitrary process, to the absolute destruction of all sin and sinful appetite in the believer's heart. Thus, then, the work of redemption on the Cross is but a step in the process of salvation, not the process itself. A vast and important step in the direction of salvation, no doubt, but still not the whole process. That process consists in the appropriation by the believer, as the root-principle of his life, of the Divine humanity in Jesus Christ. Reconciled by the Death of Jesus Christ, saved by His Life, born again by His Spirit, the whole Trinity, Father, Son, and Holy Ghost, come to him and make their abode in him, so that he becomes the holy temple of the living God. This, and no less than this, is the reason why God became man; this, and no less than this, is what is meant, in all its fulness, by the Atonement.

In our concluding lecture an endeavour will be made to put forward some considerations regarding the process of redemption which will not be liable to many of the objections successfully urged against the theory of substitution as generally stated. It is not pretended that such considerations will amount to more than suggestions tending toward the removal of certain difficulties, while at the same time maintaining unimpaired the credit of God's revealed Word. To attempt a task which has baffled the acutest and profoundest intellects in Christendom, to attempt, that is, to construct a full and exhaustive theory of Christian redemption, would be an endeavour as full of presumption as it would be foredoomed to failure. But to endeavour to remove a stumbling-block or two out of our neighbour's way, to indulge a hope that it may be permitted to contribute something, be it ever so little, toward the elucidation of a vast mystery, even though the ultimate truth on which it depends, like all other ultimate truth, be far above out of our sight,—is a more reasonable object to propose to oneself. Whether these lectures do or do not attain even this humble object, must be left to Him to whom alone it belongs to prosper or to frustrate the feeble efforts of man.

LECTURE IV.

THE VARIOUS ASPECTS OF PROPITIATION.

"*Behold the Lamb of God, which taketh away the sin of the world.*"— ST. JOHN i. 29.

THIS declaration, made by one whose special mission it was to prepare the way for Christ, contains in a brief space the whole Gospel of salvation. He who denies this denies Christ; for Christ came to take away sin, and by none other than He could sin be taken away. But when we enter upon the question, How did He take away sin? a boundless field of imagination and conjecture is opened out to us. The question is as wide as humanity. It touches man at every point of his complex being. In whatever direction he has gone wrong, in whatever way it may be possible to bring him back, there the great doctrine of Atonement comes in to indicate the force at work and the point at which it is to be applied.

We have carefully examined the teaching of Scripture on this most momentous subject; and we have also inquired how that teaching has been understood in the universal Church of Christ. What, then, is of faith on this point? Do you believe, we are asked as a test of orthodoxy, that the Death of Christ was penal and vicarious? We reply, That depends upon what is meant by the words. We say "yes," if you mean by penal that the sorrows and sufferings Christ bore were the natural consequences, or punishment, if you please, of sin;—if you mean by vicarious that by undergoing them, He saved us from undergoing something which otherwise we should have been compelled to endure. For were it not for sin, sorrow and suffering would never have existed; and therefore whosoever bears either is enduring the punishment of sin. And it is a law of nature that the consequences of a man's sin never stop short with himself, but that innocent persons are involved in such consequences. Suffering for other men's sins is a principle of humanity, and it were not unreasonable that a larger share than usual of such suffering should fall on his head who tries to remove it. But if you go further than this, if you insist upon attaching to the word "penal" the interpretation that the punishment Christ bore was not merely the consequence of sin, but the penalty due to obstinate, impenitent sinners, or a precise equivalent to it; and to the word "vicarious" the interpretation that He by bearing such punishment satisfied the Father's justice, or bore His wrath, or both, in our stead; that He thus removed from us all necessity whatever for bearing that wrath or any part of it, then, if we do not say categorically "no" to the question, we at least say that it is permissible to do so. For the supposition involves us in grave difficulties. What is the punishment due to sin? Is it death? Then Christ did not remove that punishment from us, for we all die, and death is the decreed penalty of transgression. Is it suffering? No, for we all must suffer. Is it eternal torment? Some, it is true, have gone so far as to say that Christ suffered an equivalent to this—itself, of course, He could not have suffered. But we may ask, first, What authority is there in Holy Writ for such a statement? and if such a statement be not, as it is not, to be found there, we may next ask, Who are we, to take upon ourselves to state either to what the sufferings of Christ, or the torments of the lost, are equivalent, who know nothing of either? The fact is that, here as elsewhere, men's minds are confused by the use of words in different and often contradictory significations. "Vicarious" is one of those words. The word, strictly speaking, implies substitution in another's place. Applied to the sufferings of Christ it is accurate, as we have seen, in a certain sense. He suffered, that we might not suffer. But that He was so completely our substitute that He bore precisely what we ought to have undergone, in order that we might undergo nothing whatever, is obviously an incorrect statement of the case, for then we should no longer have anything to endure, whereas, as a matter of fact, Christ's disciples must needs share His sufferings, that they may enter into His glory. "No Cross, no Crown," is so certain a truth, that it has passed into a proverb. The word "vicarious," therefore, must be employed with caution, as indicating one aspect, and only one, of Christ's Sacrifice. He suffered, it is true, that we might not suffer the extreme penalty of sin. But He did not suffer to relieve us from all suffering. On the contrary, that we may obtain the deliverance He came to bring, we must learn to suffer with Him. And therefore the illustrations of Christ's Sacrifice, drawn from the frequency of vicarious[1] suffering in the world, are beside the

---

[1] That is, suffering on account of others, but not necessarily in their stead.

point unless they remind us that suffering for others is often unavailing, until those for whom it is borne can comprehend, and, to a certain extent, can share it. The illustration of the broken-hearted mother, who suffers and dies under the burden of the sins of an undutiful son, is incomplete unless it ends with the picture of that son, reclaimed at last by the spectacle of a love steadfast unto death, casting himself on his mother's grave, and crying in agony answering to hers, "O my mother, all this thou hast endured for me." And so even the Passion of Christ is for us in vain until we have part in it; until the shadow of His Agony creeps over our soul, until our "old man is crucified with Him," and from the ashes of our dead selves there rises the "new man, which after Christ is created in righteousness and true holiness."

We believe, then, that Christ both did and suffered something instead of us. What He did instead of us is clear enough. He perfectly fulfilled the Law of God, which we have not done, and never could have done. What He suffered instead of us we do not and never shall know. His sufferings, so far as human reason may be trusted to deal with such a subject, do not seem to have been the precise equivalent of ours, for there are many pains incident to humanity which He never bore, many sufferings of the intensest kind which He did not undergo. How far these may be regarded as that filling up by the members of the sufferings of their Head of which St. Paul speaks,[1] we cannot say. But, on the other hand, His sufferings were of a kind which none of us can fully share. We can none of us estimate, as He did, the true horror and shame of the sins of a whole world. We can never

[1] Col. i. 24.

take in at a single glance, as He could, the accumulated weight of guilt, with its accompanying load of misery, which had been incurred and had been, or would hereafter have to be endured, according to God's own righteous ordinances, by those of whom He became the Representative and the Head. We may believe that He could hardly have been very Man, that He certainly could not have possessed the love and sympathy essential to perfect Manhood, had He not felt, with indescribable intensity, how vast, how terrible, these consequences of sin had been already, and would be hereafter. But we need not think it necessary to add that in this suffering of His in sympathy with those whose nature He had put on, and in nothing else, consisted the satisfaction to the Father's justice for the sins of the whole world. Still less should we undertake to balance His sufferings against those we had merited to bear, to assert either that the one were equivalent to the other, or that the exaction of such equivalent was necessary in order to manifest, or vindicate, or satisfy the Justice of the perfect and justly offended Ruler of the world.[1]

In what, then, consisted the virtue of Christ's Death? Various schools of theology, as we have seen, have given various answers to the question, and each has its objections to any solution other than its own. The question will no doubt arise in your minds, Which are you about to adopt? And my reply is, None of them, at least by itself. I cannot believe the question capable of any simple solution. Why, I would ask, may not each one of these theories be a partial answer to a question which we have just declared to be as wide as humanity, as unsearchable as the Being of

[1] Note 1.

God? Why may not each contribute its element to an explanation, which at best can be but incomplete, of that great Sacrifice of self which was the death of man to sin? If Christ be in truth, as St. John tells us He is, the Mercy-Seat where God's glory and man's offering meet,[1] can we doubt that the various lights in which we ought to view a transaction so momentous, must be practically infinite?

To some few of these I would invite your attention in this concluding lecture. I will not pretend to exhaust the subject, for I believe that it cannot be exhausted. I would not present any one of these considerations as excluding another, for I believe that they all have their place in the *rationale* of so Divine a mystery.[2] I believe that the true attitude of the believer in relation to the unfolding of the great Divine purpose of Atonement for sin ought not to be, "See how simple it is. I will explain it to you in a very few words," but rather, "O the depth of the riches both of the wisdom and knowledge of God. How unsearchable are His judgments, and His ways past finding out!"[3]

---

[1] 1 John ii. 2.

[2] I would call attention for a moment to the evidential value of this way of presenting the subject. The doctrine of Atonement, thus presented, becomes not a chain, but a network. If one single link of a chain be found defective, the chain is broken. If one or two meshes of the net give way, the net still holds. We may reject some methods of accounting for Propitiation by the Death of Christ, but there may be others which satisfy our mind. And thus this great central doctrine of the faith becomes many-sided, like those whom it concerns. It does not rest upon the acceptance or rejection of a single theological proposition, but it appeals in many ways to the sympathies of those for whom it exists. And thus it falls in, not only with the nature of man, but with the greatness of Him Who "dwelleth in the Light that no man can approach unto."

[3] Rom. xi. 33.

OF PROPITIATION.

The leading ideas contained in the Sacrifice of Christ, as Dr. McLeod Campbell in his thoughtful and original treatise points out, flow in two main channels. The Mediator between God and Man acts toward man on the part of God, and toward God on the part of man. This is the explanation of the fact that Christ is the Mercy-Seat, because in Him God and Man meet, God is Himself the Propitiatory Sacrifice. This is why the new Covenant or Agreement is made in Christ's blood, which is His Life, because God is Man and Man is God, and the mind of each is one and the same. And each of the two aspects of Christ's Propitiatory work embraces a vast number of details. In this lecture we can but select a few of these. But the more reverently and earnestly—and I may perhaps venture to add the less logically and dogmatically—the Sacrifice of Christ is regarded, the more the number of aspects in which the Passion can be regarded will multiply.

I. We have said that Christ came to act with man on behalf of God, for the one essential object of His Mission was to reveal the Father. "No man hath seen God at any time. The only begotten Son, He Who exists in the bosom of the Father, He hath revealed Him."[1] "He that hath seen Me hath seen the Father."[2] And how did He reveal Him? As Infinite Justice[3] and Infinite Love.[4] But these attributes of the Divine seem to come into collision when dealing with a fact like sin. Jesus Christ comes to clear men's minds from the perplexity into which this terrible fact has thrown them, to unfold the mystery

---

[1] ὁ ὢν εἰς τὸν κόλπον τοῦ πατρός. John i. 18.
[2] John xiv. 9; cf. xii. 45.
[3] Matt. xxiv. 45-51, xxv. 1-46; John v. 19-30, &c.
[4] John iii. 16, 17.

how God can at once be just and the justifier of those who believe in Him.[1]

1. Christ, by coming and suffering in the flesh, explains the true nature of suffering in the Divine economy. The fact of the wrath of God against sin was only too clear in itself. It was moreover "witnessed to by the law and by the prophets."[2] And thus the pain, misery, and distress in the world—the "four sore judgments" which God pronounced against Jerusalem and other nations which rebelled against Him; the sharp chastisements with which He was wont to vindicate His Law against transgressors—had brought men to regard Him as a stern Lawgiver, an unbending Judge, or a power at war with Himself, if not as a being altogether malevolent towards man. Jesus Christ, by His sufferings and death, proves to us that pain and suffering are no signs of God's anger, but of His love. Sin He hates, and pain and suffering are the signs of that hate. But they are intended not for man's harm, but for his good. They are directed against a temporary derangement of His blessed purpose, not against the beings He has made for happiness. If Scripture under the Old Testament speaks of a wrath against sinners, it also speaks of God's long-suffering and loving-kindness. Jesus Christ explains all this to us. If clouds are in the sky, yet the sun is shining behind them. If God Himself consents in sinless human shape to endure these signs of His Own Wrath, what better proof can we have that that Wrath is only Love disguised? Sorrow and suffering are but the fires whereby He designs to "purify the sons of Levi, that they may offer to Him an offering in righteousness."[3]

2. Closely allied to this consideration is another.

[1] Note 2.   [2] Rom. iii. 21.   [3] Mal. iii. 3.

From a general, we proceed to an individual application of the principle. Till Christ came, prosperity was considered a sign of God's love, adversity of His wrath. And so, abstractedly considered, it is, and ought to be. But further consideration induces us to suspend our judgment. For good and evil are strangely intermingled in this world. The punishment often seems to fall on the wrong shoulders. Is the world then a moral iniquity? Is there no righteousness to be found therein? Let Jesus Christ tell us. Individual suffering, like suffering in general, is not the sign of God's wrath but of His Love. To endure the consequences of other men's sins is the appointed discipline of the soul which makes "all things work together for good."[1] "Whom the Lord loveth He chasteneth, and scourgeth every son whom He receiveth." If He laid the sins of the world upon His Own Well-beloved Son, Who did no sin, neither was guile found in His Mouth, we can have no better proof of His tender affection than when He calls us to bear our cross after Him. Thus the riddle of the world is unriddled. The Lord of all is not unjust in causing us to suffer, but He bids us follow Christ, bids us suffer, and even die, like Him, that sorrow and suffering may cease to be.

3. Christ suffered that He might reveal the true relations of God to sin. It is a remarkable fact that the Death of Christ did emphatically "condemn sin in the flesh"[2] in the only way in which a God Who is Love could effectually condemn it. As we have already remarked, to proclaim a general amnesty to all offenders while yet they continued in sin were to put an end to all distinctions between right and wrong. But when the

---

[1] Rom. viii. 28.   [2] Rom. viii. 3.

sinless Son of God Himself dies to vindicate God's justice; when He cheerfully submits to the law that "the wages of sin is death" as the representative of all mankind, He proclaims the truth that sin is indeed a deadly thing in God's sight, while yet He makes for us a way to escape from it. His sufferings and death are the translation into the sphere of human experience of God's utter hatred and loathing of sin. It is not easy to see how we otherwise could have obtained even the faintest idea of that loathing. But when we see the eternal God Himself, made man, undergoing the sentence of sin, we see at once that not even the deepest, tenderest, most infinite love to man can stand in the way of His most absolute and emphatic condemnation of sin; nay, that this very love imperatively requires that sin should be so condemned, that its ruinous nature should be set forth to the world in the most vivid colours. It was part of God's loving purpose that men should not find it possible to conceive of Him as the antitype of that easy good-nature among men which looks lightly on sin, but that they should understand His hatred to sin to be of an intensity proportioned to the love He bears to everything that He has made.[1]

4. Another consideration, not very far removed from the former, may be drawn from the reasonableness of the requirement on God's part in order to a full and perfect reconciliation, that man shall make an adequate acknowledgment of the righteousness of God's Law, and of man's inexcusable guilt in transgressing it. An ἀδίκημα should be repaired by a δικαίωμα.[2] The advocates of the substitution theory, as we have seen, have wavered not a little in their view of the nature of the compensation offered to

[1] Note 3. [2] See p. 32.

God's justice. Now it is the punishment which offers such compensation, now it is the obedience of Christ. Many who would stumble at the former alternative will see no difficulty in the latter. Man must suitably acknowledge his offence before he is readmitted to favour. The majesty of law must be vindicated that we may learn henceforward not to offend. Not only must man cheerfully submit himself to the necessity of proclaiming God's Righteousness in annexing penalties to sin, but we may even believe that God may righteously require as a condition of reconciliation that he should do so. God may reasonably ask that even righteous man, if He becomes the advocate of His race, should bow to the law which decrees that pain and death are the just lot of humanity, that all men may thus learn how real God's condemnation of sin is. For Christ undertook not only to obey God Himself, but to redeem those who had not done so.[1] Could He offer adequate reparation for them without submitting Himself to the law as it affected the guilty as well as the innocent? Must He not accept the position of lost sinners ere He could retrieve their fallen condition? Is it not thus that He could best display to man the Righteousness of God? And there is a yet further reason why it should be so. Jesus did not come to show men a way whereby they could attain to God's favour without obeying God. He did not come, as we are so apt to persuade ourselves, to make reconciliation *for* them, without making it *in* them. By His Cross and Passion He taught them how they might learn to obey Him, even by imbibing His Spirit of full and absolute obedience to every jot and tittle of God's Righteous Law. For propitiation does not consist in God's absolving us

[1] Note 4.

from obedience to His commands. On the contrary, He will not, He cannot, let one single precept of His Wisdom fall to the ground. Jesus Christ, therefore, comes to raise us to the level of God's commands, not to let them down to ours. Jesus Christ came to proclaim that "the law is holy, and the commandment holy, just, and good." He came to teach us that only by obedience to that Righteous Law could we attain salvation; that God not only hates sin Himself, but He requires us to hate it also. God is not reconciled to us until, by faith in Him, this His Mind in regard to sin is reflected in our hearts.

5. Lastly (and the thought brings us infinitely near to our first consideration on this head), the sufferings of Jesus Christ were the plainest and clearest manifestations possible of the Love of God, I may say the only possible way in which that Love, in all its fulness, could be made comprehensible to mankind. Jesus came to manifest the Father to men. And how did He manifest Him? By the terrors of God's wrath against impenitent sinners? By pestilences and famines and plagues and diseases and death inflicted upon man for sin? No, the Lord was not in the earthquake, in the mighty wind that rent the mountains, or in the fire, but in the still small voice of tender and forbearing love. He came preaching the Gospel to the poor, healing the broken-hearted, preaching deliverance to the captives, recovery of sight to the blind, liberty to the bruised. He came taking away men's sicknesses, bearing their infirmities, sympathising with their sorrows. He came enduring contradiction of sinners. His yearning heart wept over the city that knew not the time of its visitation. And He "bowed His meek head to mortal pain," He felt the weight of the world's sins as though

they were His own, He stooped to death itself, and that the death of the Cross, and thus He made known to men the nature of God. Was it possible in any other way to enable men to measure the depth of Divine tenderness and compassion, than by dying to save them? We cannot express His witness for the Father among men in worthier or more touching words than those which He Himself uttered, "Greater love hath no man than this, that he lay down his life for his friends."

II. Thus we have seen, in very brief and imperfect outline, some of the ways in which God's character is revealed to mankind by the sufferings and Death of Christ. We proceed to ask how, in those same sufferings and Death, man is brought into union with God. We are apt to think of man as making an external satisfaction, through a substitute. The real truth is, that Christ makes satisfaction for man by bringing his whole being into harmony with the mind of God. When we speak of satisfaction we do not speak of satisfaction to God's Wrath, for that can only be appeased by taking away its cause. We do not speak of satisfaction to His Justice, by the exaction of an adequate penalty, for it seems doubtful whether the exaction of any penalty whatever can be a satisfaction to justice, properly so called. But it is to His Eternal Righteousness that satisfaction is made; and this can only be satisfied when man is as Righteous as God Himself, when the mind and will of man and of God are one; when the whole being of the creature is the mirror of the perfections of his Creator.

1. First and foremost, the Passion of Christ is, as Dr. McLeod Campbell has most felicitously expressed it, the "Amen of humanity" to the righteous judgment of God.

God has decreed that "the soul that sinneth, it shall die."[1] Jesus Christ, as the representative of sinners, the one true and perfect man, presents, on the part of mankind, a full admission of the justice of the sentence. Man has sinned, man has deserved to die; and He Who takes upon Him the nature of man, He Who is actually *the* Man, dies in order that the justice of that sentence may be most fully recognised and proclaimed.[2]

2. The death of Christ, and in this view in a special way His sufferings, are the adequate acknowledgment of the guilt of sin, the full and entire repentance (by which word I mean change of mind and purpose) on the part of man for his sins, which, as I have already said, it seems reasonable to suppose that God must receive on man's part, unless He would reveal Himself to us as One Who made light of sin. It was necessary to man's salvation that the real enormity of sin should not be concealed. And for this reason Jesus Christ came at once to reveal and acknowledge it. His sufferings were the measure and the expression of His sense of that enormity. Suffering in man is, as we have seen, the expression of God's hatred of sin. The purer, the holier the man, the more intense such suffering will be. It was the very perfection of Christ's Humanity, the very completeness of His sinlessness, which caused His sufferings on behalf of sin to be so great. He was true Man, and therefore He felt for us as only true Man can. But our imperfect, sin-stained natures can have no idea how the realisation of our actual condition, the fixed purpose to present on our behalf a full acknowledgment of it to God, would affect a perfect human soul. We have learned by experience the danger

[1] Ezek. viii. 4, 20.   [2] Note 5.

of illustrations of things Divine by things human. And yet, as regards Christ's sufferings, some light may be thrown on their nature by the figure of the head of a clan, himself intensely loyal to his king, yet who finds that his clan have been involved in rebellion. The more intense and perfect his loyalty, the more thorough his nobleness of heart and affection for his people, the more inexcusable and flagrant the rebellion of those for whom he pleads, the more acute would be his agony, as their representative and head. Nothing would be more true to human nature in the best sense of those words, than that the conflict between loyalty to his king and affection for his vassals should induce him to offer his life for theirs, to ask that the punishment they deserved should be inflicted on him. Human justice, you say, forbids the granting of such a request. No doubt; but the conscience of man feels at once how true to all that is best in humanity is the fact that it is made. That Jesus Christ should suffer intensely on our behalf; that He should offer His Life for ours, is the very clearest proof that He is true man, that He is all that man ought to be, that before God and man alike He manifests that loyalty and affection to God and His brethren, which is the true attitude of man toward his Maker and his kind. And if we stumble at the further thought that God should accept His Death on our behalf, it is only because that Death has been too much pressed in the light of a satisfaction to the claims of inexorable justice. Regard it as the expression to the uttermost of a Perfect Being's abhorrence of evil—the bringing down to the level of human conceptions of the relation of God to sin; look upon it as His eternal proclamation of the truth that sin in itself is utterly unpardonable, abominable, intolerable, that nothing short of its utter abolition and extirpation, its absolute removal from the whole human race, could satisfy the demands of God or secure the happiness of man, and we can see how, as perfect man, He would desire thus to die for His brethren, as well as how God, Whose Mind was one here as elsewhere with that of the Perfect Man, would permit, and even desire that He should do so. And if we still stumble at God's acceptance of His offer, if we feel that an offer of this kind must be at once rejected by every upright man, we may remember that this is because life once taken can never by man be restored. To us death is irremediable. But to God it is not so. Jesus Christ says of His perishable human life (to be distinguished, as we have seen, from the Divine ζωή), "I have power to lay it down, and I have power to take it again." Nay, He even lays down the principle, which we can now understand in the light of the Cross, that to lose one's life is in truth to find it. In accordance with this principle, we find that God not only can restore, He has restored to us a thousandfold the life which He took. And He has restored it by taking it. The Act which manifested before God, angels and men, that true man hated sin as God Himself hated it, which proclaimed in this most practical way that death was the only true penalty for sin, was the means whereby sin should itself be slain, the only true pathway to any true or real life for man. If this still seem to us extravagant; if the Sacrifice demanded still seem to us excessive, let us remember that, sinners as we are, we cannot understand as a perfect being can, how terrible a blemish in God's fair world sin really is. How great the sacrifice it required, how stern and yet how moving a proof of its enormity was necessary, we perhaps shall never fully know. In this life at least, let us be content to learn how emphatically Christ "condemned sin in the flesh," and let us seek the strength He gives to enable us to condemn it also.[1]

3. Our next consideration is, that Christ not only admits the justice of God's Law by submitting to it in the name of us all, not only condemns sin in the name of humanity, but He identifies Himself with those to whom He came.[2] He stoops to their level, that He may raise them to His. He endures all the temptations to which humanity is prone. He accepts all the conditions sin has brought upon us; all the misery and wretchedness, the dull depression of heart, the sense of humiliation, the feeling of loneliness and abandonment. He does not refuse to experience the fear of death, the promptings of despair, the anguish of approaching dissolution, yea, even the rending asunder of soul and body. From these deepest depths of the misery caused by sin He rescues us by submitting to descend to them. Thus He vanquishes both sin itself, and the misery it has caused. Thus He brings manhood victorious out of every conflict sin has brought on the human soul. There is nothing man has to suffer which He has not endured. He was "in all points tempted like as we are, yet without sin."[3] And had He not been so tempted, He had not redeemed us. The price that He pays for us is obedience to the law, not only for Himself, but for us also. Nor is this difficult to understand. He cannot save us from the penalties of sin without first bearing them Himself, and thus showing us how to bear them. He cannot teach us how to come out of

---

[1] Note 6.   [2] Heb. ii. 17, 18.   [3] Heb. iv. 15.

such terrible conflicts victorious without going through them on our behalf. If He reverses the consequences of sin by enduring them, it is to show us that we, too, shall best undo the work of the evil one by submitting cheerfully to the burden man has laid on his own shoulders. It is hard, no doubt, to shake ourselves free from the thought that redemption consists in paying a price *for* us, instead of doing a work *in* us. But in truth Christ redeems us by transforming us into the Image of Himself. He delivers us from the consequences of sin by triumphing over them first for us and then in us. He displays to us first, under the form of man, the Mind of God regarding the miseries under which humanity labours. And then He produces in us, by the working of His Spirit, a mind that answers to the Divine. Pain and misery are evils; they are terrible evils; they originated in our defiance of God's will. But if they are to be overcome they must be overcome, not by flying from them, but by looking them in the face. Here as elsewhere the saying is true, "Resist the devil and he will flee from you." You are tempted, you are in anguish of soul or body, you are miserable, forlorn, despairing, hated and despised by mankind. You are racked in every limb with pain; you are drawing near to that which in all appearance is your last end; you must soon bid a final farewell to the world you have loved so dearly. Yet if you have the Mind of Jesus Christ you may be severely tried, but you are not overwhelmed. Agony, confusion, doubt, despair, cannot fail to dog our steps in a world of sin. But they have no power to fetter the believing soul. In the worst and utmost assaults of the powers of darkness, you may suffer cruelly, but in the depths of your heart you feel you are a free man. Christ has vanquished Death and Satan. They may rage henceforth, but they cannot destroy. There is no depth of human sorrow to which He has not descended, and from which He has not risen triumphant to the highest heaven. Unite yourself with Him by faith, and His triumph is yours. You are redeemed from the curse of the law by Him Who has borne the curse for you. "In all these things we are more than conquerors, through Him that loved us."[1]

4. Nor have we yet exhausted the aspects in which the Cross of Christ presents itself as the reconciliation of man to God. Christ, we are taught to say in our Communion Office, " offers a full, perfect, and sufficient sacrifice for the sins of the whole world." Now what were the main features of the sacrifices of the ancient world as they presented themselves to us in a former lecture?[2] They were these, (1) the offering of our best, and (2) the identifying ourselves in spirit with that which we offered. And is not Christ our very best, the very crown and glory of our humanity? Was not His Sacrifice the offer of a perfect human Life to God? And does it not need that we should by faith identify ourselves with Him, that our mind toward sin and toward righteousness, and toward God, the Author of all righteousness, should by faith become one with His, before His redemption is efficacious for our salvation? We must dismiss from our minds, let me repeat once more, if we would understand the Passion aright, all thought of Christ's Death as a mere propitiation *for* us; the Atonement involves a change wrought *in* us by faith in the Blood of Christ. It is not until, by God's infinite mercy, His Eternal Spirit has brought our minds into full accord with the Will of God,

---

[1] Rom. viii. 37.   [2] Lect. II.

that the Atonement wrought out by Christ on behalf of mankind can be said to be fully effected for ourselves. It is not until we offer and present Christ to the Father as the very pattern of all we ought and wish to be; until we strive from our inmost souls to be conformed to the Spirit of that "Lamb without blemish and without spot,"[1] that we know anything of the salvation that is in Him.

5. One other point I cannot altogether leave unnoticed. St. Paul speaks of the death of Christ as being the unification of mankind.[2] A little consideration will show us how. "One touch of nature makes the whole world kin," says the poet. It is just that "touch of nature" which we see in Jesus on the Cross. In His suffering, dying, undergoing in all things the lot of sinful men, we feel that He is one of ourselves. Between us and Him there is no "great gulf fixed." We cannot look upon Him as too far above us, Who condescended thus to share our lot with us. Like the father and law-giver in the old heathen story, He offers to share the punishment of His guilty son.[3] And it is this which has given our religion its indescribable power to touch the hearts of men. "I, if I be lifted up from the earth, will draw all men unto Me," says the Saviour, and even He never uttered a truer word. The strength of the attraction lies in the appeal to the common sentiments of a common nature. The "darkest hour" of human trial and despair has, as the poet reminds us, "more power for comfort than an angel's mirth."[4] But Jesus Christ not only draws us near to Himself, but to one another. God has suffered; the endurance of suffering is henceforth fellowship with God. But it is also fellowship with man. God and man are then only recon-

---

[1] 1 Pet. i. 19.   [2] Eph. ii. 14.   [3] Note 7.   [4] Note 8.

ciled when all men are one in Him. "Bear ye one another's burdens, and so fulfil the law of Christ."[1] "Beloved, if God so loved us, we ought also to love one another."[2] We are only redeemed from sin when we recognise in our conduct the truth that "we are all baptized into one Body," and have "been made to drink into One Spirit."[3] We are only redeemed when we have cast out all selfish aims, all thoughts of benefiting ourselves at the expense of our neighbours; when we have learned that only by bearing the infirmities, the sorrows, the sins of other people, can we manifest the fact that we are reconciled to God. This is why we could only be truly reconciled to Him by the Blood of His Son Jesus Christ.

6. Jesus Christ came to destroy death, and "bring life and immortality to light through the Gospel."[4] What could be more in accordance with reason, than that, as Athanasius tells us, Christ, being Himself immortal through the union of the Godhead and the Manhood, should give His Body to death, in order that, when He had preserved It from corruption, and raised It to eternal life, He should impart that perfected humanity to us, and raise us also, through the vital union which faith produces between us and Him. Nor need we exclude from this view the striking teaching of William Law that in thus giving His Body to death, Jesus slew our "old man," which He had taken of His earthly parent, in order that by His resurrection a "new man" might be raised up, from which all "likeness of sinful flesh" was for ever removed. The death of Christ was the death of sin and hell and all things sin had

---

[1] Gal. vi. 2.
[2] 1 John iv. 11.
[3] 1 Cor xii. 13.
[4] 2 Tim. i. 10.

brought into the world.¹ In it "we all died;"² He "tasted death for every man."³ But that Flesh, which was doomed to death, He "gave for the life of the world."⁴ That glorious Body "saw no corruption,"⁵ but exalted and purified from all that was (not corrupt, but) corruptible, It was "raised for our justification,"⁶ to whom Its glorified Life was to be imparted. And so, though like His, our mortal body dies, it is destined by reason of our inward and spiritual union with Him, to rise again like His, and to live in uncorrupted and incorruptible beauty for evermore.⁷

7. One consideration more, and only one, I will advance before I conclude. The endurance of sorrow, suffering, even death itself, is absolutely necessary to the highest conception of humanity. What we understand by nobleness can have no existence, save in a world where sorrow and sin exist, nor can it find a place in any heart save that of the man who braves danger, who freely exposes life at the call of duty. This principle was dimly recognised in the old heathen times. The names of Leonidas, of Decius, of Regulus, were ever green in the memory of the ancient world. But what was rare among them, among Christians has become common. We may get so used to the change that we fail to notice it, but the change has taken place nevertheless. Thousands of men now brave danger, not merely from the shame of being branded as cowards, not only in the fierce excitement of the battle-field, but calmly and resolutely, and from a simple sense of duty. No more glorious sight was ever seen than the soldiers at the wreck of the *Birkenhead*, standing firm at the word of command,

---

¹ Heb. ii. 14.   ² 2 Cor. v. 14.   ³ Heb. ii. 9.
⁴ John vi. 51.   ⁵ Acts ii. 31, xiii. 37.   ⁶ Rom. iv. 25.
⁷ Note 9.

and sinking calmly beneath the waves while the women and children were placed in safety in the boats. And quite as noble, though not so striking to the imagination, is the life of the minister of Christ who spends a lifetime in the foulest and most noisome districts of our large towns, devoting himself to a living death if only he can make the lost and degraded around him a trifle better than they were.[1] Such, too, is the conduct of the physician, in his way no less a minister of Christ, who exposes himself freely to the danger of infection and death, content if by so doing he may be enabled to diminish in some degree the sum of human suffering. If, then, Jesus Christ is to act on our behalf with the Father of all mankind; if He is to display before God the realisation of the true idea of humanity, He must be the type of all that is highest and noblest in the race; He must be our example in heroic devotion, in courage, in endurance of all that is possible for our neighbour's sake. And so He is the true mercy-seat, the true meeting-point of God and man. As He manifests the Father's love to man, so He manifests man in his highest perfection to God, when He fulfils His own saying, " Greater love hath no man than this, that a man lay down his life for his friends."

Such, my brethren, are some of the aspects in which the Redeemer's work presents itself to our minds. I may venture to add, some of the *necessary* aspects in which it presents itself. For as we have seen, it were impossible for God to pardon sin without marking in some way the tremendous gravity of a deliberate infraction of His moral laws. Herein consists the necessity of Christ's Death. It is not only that without it we could neither understand

[1] Note 10.

how God looked upon sin, nor upon suffering; how He could be just in dealing with individuals as He does, or how He could at once be perfect love and the avenger of sin. But we are told that a price was paid for our redemption, that the just suffered on behalf of the unjust. And we seek for an explanation which shall be in harmony with our sense of moral fitness and spiritual truth. We find it in the intense reality of Christ's humanity; in His entire and absolute identification of Himself with us, in the perfect brotherliness of His sympathy, necessary in One Who was to be the embodiment in a human form of Divine love. We find it moreover in His vivid realisation of the fact that sin was the one bitter drop in the cup of the universe; the one plague spot in all that God had created; the cause of all the misery and pain in the world; and therefore the one thing to be hated, and fought against and rooted out and abolished for ever and ever. It was only the recognition of this fact by One Who had not brought His Own misery upon Himself; it was only this wondrous combination of perfect manhood with a perfect realisation of man's actual present condition; it was only this emphatic witness at once to God's Righteousness and man's corruption that could reconcile man to God, and yet preserve intact God's eternal condemnation of all that is evil.

This is the objective necessity for Christ's Death. There is also a subjective necessity for it. There is in man, however he may seek to slur it over, or to get rid of its burden—there is in the depth of his heart a feeling that he *cannot* make satisfaction to God for his own sin.[1] This is at the bottom of all those gloomy legends

---
[1] Note II.

of the vengeance of the Furies which disturbed the minds of men in days gone by. This is the cause of that haunting dread of punishment which Plutarch describes in his time as driving men to distraction. This is at the root of all the austerities, penances, macerations of the flesh which have been practised by heathen and Christian alike. And yet it has ever been felt that all these severities are in vain. Nothing can satisfy the human heart but the feeling that a Saviour has come, Who has discharged the debt that no man was ever able to pay, Who has "fulfilled all righteousness" not for Himself only but for all that ever were born, Who has submitted to the law as it affects not only innocent, but guilty man. Forward to Him they looked in the dim twilight of the ages before Christ. Backward to His Cross they have turned their eyes with infinite comfort ever since He manifested Himself to the world. It is this doctrine of Satisfaction that is the strength of Christianity. Remove it; supply its place by a proclamation of pardon, made by one who is a perfect example, and you throw men back into all the perplexities from which Christ has set them free. But tell them that in trying to make satisfaction for their own misdeeds they are only attempting a hopeless task; tell them that the satisfaction has been already made, and that they have but to live by faith in the Spirit of Him Who made it, and they breathe again. A man has not to address himself to the hopeless task of clearing old scores before he can regard himself as free. He is free already. He has but to stand fast in the freedom in which Christ has freed him, he has but to imbibe the Spirit of his Master, he has but to "walk in love, as Christ also has loved us, and given Himself an offering to God for us as a sweet-smelling savour," and he is safe. Such a man does not desire to inquire too curiously *how* he is freed. He is not concerned to frame a theory of redemption. All he knows is that Christ died for him, and that is enough. He feels that the precious Life thus offered on man's behalf were a ransom great enough for the sins of a thousand worlds. He feels that that most blessed Death was for us the destruction of death, that in it the heart of man beat in unison with that of his Maker, that it was to our feeble humanity the highest possible manifestation of the ideal of man, as well as of the love of our Father in heaven.[1]

[1] Note 12.

NOTES.

LECTURE I.

Note 1, p. 2.

Herbert Spencer, *First Principles*, ch. iii., On Ultimate Scientific Ideas.

Note 2, p. 2.

Dean Mansel, *The Limits of Religious Thought Examined*, being the Bampton Lectures for 1858.

Note 3, p. 2.

Mr. Herbert Spencer, in the chapter above quoted, and Dean Mansel, in the second and third of his Bampton Lectures, comes to the same conclusion on this point, although they draw opposite inferences from it.

Note 4, p. 6.

I use the words "propitiation for sin," rather than "Atonement," because the latter is invariably confounded in the minds of mankind with the Sacrificial Act which was the crown and completion of our Lord's atoning work. See Lect. III., where this word is defined. Also Calmet, *Dictionary of the Bible*, and Kitto, *Biblical Cyclopædia*, s.v. *Atonement*.

Note 5, p. 7.

"We protest, with a strong abhorrence, against the dreadful views which are given concerning God's inability to forgive, of the justice of the Father horribly satisfied by the substitution of the innocent for the sins of the guilty." Thom, *Lecture on the Practical Importance of the Unitarian Controversy*, p. 31. This lecture was delivered in 1839.

Note 6, p. 7.

That the human element strongly predominates in many, if not most, attempts to formulate a satisfactory theory of the Atonement—satisfactory, that is, of course, to the human intellect—is unfortunately too clear. The most fantastic opinions have been propounded on the point. The Lutheran divine, Philippi, for instance, lays it down that Christ suffered eternal death as truly as the damned, because He, as God, could suffer *intensivè* in a short space of time, what the weak capacity of ordinary human nature requires to be extended over an infinite period. The theory is not only absolutely without warrant from Scripture, but it requires us to accept as a foundation the doctrine of the passibility of God. The Catholic doctrine has been that Jesus Christ could only suffer as man. Another theologian, Cotta, puts the matter thus: that Jesus did not suffer infernal pains, but what might reasonably be considered as equivalent to infernal pains.

For these statements I am indebted to a work of rare ability and research recently published, *Lectures on the Humiliation of Christ*, by A. B. Bruce, D.D., being the Cunningham Lectures for 1875. It is to be lamented that this author, who displays a Catholic spirit, and an acquaintance and sympathy with early and mediæval theology very uncommon in writers of his communion, should feel himself bound by the chains of the

Westminster Confession. His toleration and candour never fail him, save when members of the Scottish communions stray from the paths of orthodoxy. He has not a hard word for any one among the vast range of authors whom his erudition has led him to consult, save those two remarkable men, Edward Irving and McLeod Campbell. To them it must be confessed he does but scant justice. He can see nothing but "eccentricity" in the thoughtful treatise of the latter divine. Yet that treatise contains nothing more surprising than the following passages from Dr. Bruce's work: "Summing up, then, the elements of value in our Lord's atoning death as inductively ascertained from Scripture, we get this formula, expressed *in mathematical language,* though the thing to be estimated is a *moral quantity not admitting of mathematical measurement.* The value of Christ's sacrifice *was equal to His divine dignity, multiplied by His perfect obedience, multiplied by His divine love, multiplied by suffering in body and soul* carried to the uttermost limits of what a sinless being can experience." Lectures, p. 391. The italics are my own. Again, p. 352, he says, "What is meant by the Catholic doctrine is not transference of guilt and moral turpitude, but simply of *legal liability.*" He does, however (p. 362), speak of the πολυποίκιλος σοφία of God, and he admits that the doctrine of Atonement has many sides, an admission clearly involved in the first of the passages here cited. The Atonement is there most truly represented as a process infinitely more complex than the simple appeasing of the Father's wrath, or satisfaction of His justice, caused by our Saviour consenting to endure, as our substitute, the punishment of our sins.

NOTE 7, p. 8.

John Owen, *The death of death in the death of Christ.* Collected Works, vol. v. p. 366. In his *Vindiciae Evangelicae* (ch. 27, Of the Satisfaction of Christ) he lays down the following theorems: (1) that there was a voluntary concurrence and distinct consent "of the Father and the Sonne for the Accomplishment of the worke of our peace, and bringing us to God." (2) That "for the Accomplishment of this work, the Father who is principall in the Covenant . . . requires of the Lord Jesus Christ his Sonne, that he shall *do* that which upon consideration of his Justice, Glory, and Honour, was necessary to be done for bringing about the end proposed." Among the things necessary to be done we find, (3) "that he should suffer and undergoe, what in justice is due to him, that he should deliver." (4) "The Lord Jesus Christ accepts of the Condition and the Promise, and voluntarily undertakes the worke, Ps. xl. 7, 8." Lastly, it is necessary that "on the *one side* the *promiser* do approve and accept of the performance of the condition prescribed and the *undertaker demand* and lay clayme to the *promises* made, and thereupon the *common end* designed be accomplished and fulfilled." Christ redeemed us, he goes on to argue, by paying the price due for sin. Now the "Justice of God, or the just and *Holy Will* of God, requires punishment for sinne" (ch. 28). Christ's death he asserts to be the price of our redemption; that if God was "pacatus et placatus" He had been "provoked," that "anger" is but an accommodation to our weakness, that what is meant is the "obstacles in God's nature" whereby He cannot be satisfied with sinners; that to die for us must mean to die in our stead; that a substitution or commutation is clearly taught by Scripture (ch. 30). This treatise was published in 1655 (my quotations are made from the original edition), and is dedicated to the Lord Protector's Council of State. It is a work of great learning and intellectual power, and is written in answer to Socinus and his English disciples. But it is unduly scholastic in tone, and its deductions from the text of Scripture itself, though unquestionably showing logical grasp, require, like other scientific theories, to be tested by application to the facts of the case. I have taken no notice of the predestinarian doctrines, either of Owen or Edwards. But they form a marked feature in their system. Thus Owen, denying that Christ died for all, declares that "to affirm Christ to die for all men is the readiest way to prove that He died for no man in the sense Christians have hitherto understood." Collected Works, vol. v. p. 391.

How far modern Nonconformity has departed from this standpoint may be seen by the following extract from a thoughtful sermon by the late Rev. T. Binney, of the Weigh House Chapel, London Bridge. He describes Divine Love and human sinfulness as reconciled by the obedience or righteousness τοῦ ἑνός. (*Sermons.* Second Series. No. II. Reconciliation.) He further teaches that there were two reconciliations, first God in Christ, reconciling the world unto Himself, and second Christ reconciling man to God, by obedience, though his language on the second point is by no means clear. But he wisely goes on to say, "We may not be able to explain what the mysterious statements we have referred to mean." Dr. Binney, though a Congregationalist, preached this sermon in the Wesleyan Chapel, City Road, on October 31, 1866.

That some modification of the language of the earlier Calvinist divines had become necessary in consequence of the force of Unitarian objections is shown by Dr. McLeod Campbell's citations from a later school of Calvinist theology which has arisen in the present century. This school teaches that an atonement is rendered necessary, not by the necessity of exact personal justice being meted out to every man, but in order that the general character of God's dealings, as the moral governor of the world, should be vindicated, that none might excuse their sin on the ground that God was indifferent to it. And with regard to the imputation of sin, a man is neither pronounced, nor made, just, but simply treated as such, on account of the public vindication of God's Righteousness involved in the Sacrifice of Christ. Such is the teaching of Dr. Payne, and of the late well-known Nonconformist divine, Dr. Pye Smith. See McLeod Campbell, *On the Nature of the*

Atonement, ch. iv. Dr. Binney, we have seen, has wisely declined to pledge himself to any theory on the subject.

NOTE 8, p. 9.

History of Redemption, Period II. Part II. Sec. 4. (vol. v. of Collected Works, p. 158.)

NOTE 9, p. 9.

The Wisdom of God displayed in the Way of Salvation. Sec. 1, 2. (Collected Works, vol. v. pp. 328, 329.)

NOTE 10, p. 9.

Miscellaneous Remarks on Satisfaction for Sin. Vol. VIII. p. 481.) It is worthy of note that Edwards seems to regard the doctrine of the Divinity of Christ as depending upon the Satisfaction made by Christ on the Cross instead of maintaining the converse doctrine, as the Fathers generally do. " Christ became incarnate, or, which is the same thing, He became man, *to put Himself in a capacity for working out our redemption.*" *Hist. of Redemption*, Period II. Part I. The italics are mine. Similarly the Resurrection of Christ depends on the same Satisfaction. "The resurrection and ascension of Christ were requisite in order to the *success* of His purchase." *Ibid.* Period III. Sec. 2.

" His Resurrection was necessary in order to Christ's obtaining the end and effect of His purchase of Redemption." *Ibid.*

NOTE 11, p. 10.

" The plain scriptural notion of justification is pardon, the forgiveness of sins." Wesley, *Serm.* V., Justification by Faith (Ed. 1771).

"God imputes our sins or the guilt of them to Christ; He consented to be responsible for them, to suffer the punishment due to them." *The Scripture doctrine of Imputed Sin and Righteousness.* Works, vol. 21, p. 379.

He says that the word *Nasa* means (1) to take up somewhat, as on one's shoulders; (2) to bear or carry something weighty, as a porter does a burden; (3) to take away; and in all these senses it is here applied to the Son of God. *Ibid.*

"His sufferings were the penal effects of our sins" (p. 380). "Every chastisement is for some fault. That laid on Christ was not for His own, but for ours." *Ibid.*

Note 12, p. 10.

Skeletons for Sermons. St. Matthew xxvii. 26–31.

Note 13, p. 11.

Ibid. Rom. iii. 24–26.

Note 14, p. 11.

He "must bear all our sins had merited." Shame, misery, death, the damnation of hell, "*as far as was necessary for our redemption.*" The "great leading points of His sufferings and our deserts do fully correspond with each other." "Thus did He not merely die in our stead, 'the just for the unjust,' as a common victim in the place of the offender, but He fully discharged our debt in every particular, *so that neither law nor justice can demand anything further at our hands.*" Simeon's *Skeletons for Sermons.* St. Matt. xxvii. 26–31.

"There was a necessity on the part of God, as the moral governor of the world, that His justice should be satisfied for our violations of the law. This was done through the atoning blood of Jesus." *Ibid.*, Rom. iii. 24–26.

"That blood which satisfied Divine Justice." "When Christ has paid our debt, and we in consequence of that payment expect our discharge, we may expect it even on the footing of justice itself." *Ibid.* Yet Mr. Simeon is conscious that this statement of the case does not exhaust the truth of this Divine Mystery. Elsewhere he uses different language. "Reconciliation," he says in the *Skeletons* on Rom. v. 11, "has been purchased for men *by Christ's obedience unto death.*" There is an ambiguity in this phrase. It may either mean Christ's willingness to die, or His willingness to include even the extreme penalty of death in His obedience. In the first case the expression implies the theory of substitution. In the second it falls in with the theory that Christ died as our Representative, and as fulfilling God's requirements on our behalf.

NOTE 15, p. 11.

Guesses at Truth, by Julius and Augustus W. Hare, cited by Mr. Greg in his *Creed of Christendom.* As I have said, I cannot find the passage, and it does not seem in accordance with the usually thoughtful and measured language of these two divines. But to show how deeply the idea had rooted itself in popular theology, I may cite the following passage from the late Dean Alford's *Hulsean Lectures.* He would no doubt have repudiated such language in his later years. Nevertheless the passage is worth noting, as a proof how strong a hold the theory I have mentioned, without the limitations which keen intellects like those of Owen and Edwards had found it necessary to fence it in, had obtained on the mind of the last generation. "I see the congregation of Israel waiting, and intently gazing on the slaughtered animals now disposed in death on God's altar. Suddenly the fire of wrath comes forth from the holy place. The victims are consumed; the people shout, and fall on their faces. What did they see in this Divine act which thus gave them occasion for joy and adoration? What, but that the eternal punishment of sin after death had also descended on the substitute, and was removed away from them? But the consumption of the victims themselves could not be this vengeance. The mind of the worshipper was again directed to an infliction, in the purposes of God, of the extreme fury of the Divine wrath upon another and greater substitute." *Hulsean Lectures*, 1842, p. 53. And again, "This (*i.e.* redemption) had been brought about by the substitution of one for themselves ... who should for them bear the infliction of the Divine wrath" (p. 54). Again (Lect. IV., "The Stricken Substitute"), "The faithful Jew saw in sacrifice a representation of the Divine wrath inflicted on his substitute the Messiah" (p. 69). And once more (p. 71), "They involved the striking down of the substitute by the wrath of Jehovah."

NOTE 16, p. 11.

University Sermons, 1859–72, by the Rev. E. B. Pusey, D.D. Sermon on the Doctrine of the Atonement, pp. 234, 245, 246. But Dr. Pusey disclaims the belief (1) that God, in thus redeeming man, acted by any *necessity* (p. 235); (2) that though "sin has a sort of infinity of evil," we are bound therefore to contend that it demands an infinite satisfaction (p. 236); while (3) he declares that "it would be heresy to represent God the Son as more loving to us than God the Father," for "our redemption was equally the fruit of the love of the Father and of the Son" (p. 239). "This, then," he sums up, "is what is meant by the doctrine of satisfaction: not that God was under any necessity to redeem man, but that, if He did, for the redemption of the whole race of man there was needed a Divine Redeemer" (p. 241).

NOTE 17, p. 11.

A careful scrutiny of the preceding and succeeding notes may serve to establish this truth. For (1) in the scheme of theology which we have examined, everything, even Christ's Divinity itself, is made to depend upon the doctrine of satisfaction to the Father's wrath or justice, "the exchange of one person's suffering for another person's suffering," as Professor Smeaton puts it in his *Doctrine of the Atonement* (p. 160). This, and not the regeneration of humanity through the participation in Christ's Perfect Manhood, is made the centre of the Gospel system. And (2) we can see how a strong recoil from this doctrine of satisfaction to the outraged justice of the Father by the substitution for us of the Divine Son, has led Socinus and his followers to deny any satisfaction or propitiation whatever, and to explain away any passage of Scripture which speaks of a price paid or redemption effected. How distinctly the doctrine of satisfaction to God's wrath is still formulated may be seen by a quotation from Professor Dewar's work on the Atonement. He speaks of the time "when God, as the offended Moral Governor and Judge, thus dealt with Christ and inflicted upon Him the punishment of our sins." *The Atonement*, p. 226.

NOTE 18, p. 13.

Covetus is stated by Socinus to hold " Communis et orthodoxa sententia, Jesum Christum ideo servatorem nostrum esse quia divinae justitiae, per quam peccatores damnari merebamur, pro peccatis nostris plene satisfecerit, quae satisfactio per fidem imputatur nobis ex dono Dei credentibus.

"Ego vero censeo (says Socinus), et orthodoxam sententiam esse arbitror, Jesum Christum ideo servatorem nostrum esse, quia salutis aeternae viam nobis *annuntiaverit, confirmaverit*, et in sua ipsius persona cum vitae exemplo tum ex mortuis resurgendo, manifeste ostenderit, vitamque aeternam nobis ei fidem habentibus ipse daturus sit. Divinae autem justitiae, per quam peccatores damnari mereremur, pro peccatis nostris neque illum satisfecisse, neque, ut satisfieret, opus fuisse affirmo." Pp. 1, 2. *De J. C. Servatore Nostro* (ed. 1594).

NOTES TO LECTURE I.

We may observe here how the difficulty of the problem is complicated by the uncertainty of the meaning of δικαιοσύνη and *justitia*. Socinus opposes them to wickedness, and regards them as equivalent to *rectitudo* or *aequitas;* denying that they can legitimately be opposed to mercy. The difficulty is increased for an Englishman by the fact that righteousness and justice are supposed to mean two different things in our language, whereas in Greek and Latin the two ideas were expressed by the same word. Yet as a matter of fact there can be no righteousness wherein justice is not included.

Socinus (p. 11) urges that Divine justice *can* forgive sinners who truly repent. A mediator, according to Socinus (ch. VII.), does not in Scripture signify one who reconciles persons at variance, or at least he denies that this is its chief signification. His view is that it means merely *one who stands between.* See Gal. iii. 19 (where Calvin translates it *internuncium*). He deals with less success with 1 Tim. ii. 5; Heb. viii. 6, ix. 15, xii. 24. From 2 Cor. v. he draws the conclusion that Christ did not appease God, but manifested Him as appeased. Ch. VIII. (p. 55), but see Theodoret *in loc.* Reconciliation (ch. VIII. p. 62) is not properly made by Christ's blood, but by Him. Again, p. 63, it is we who are reconciled to God, not He to us, by Christ. But Socinus, although a clear and accurate thinker, is driven by the necessity of his position to a manifest wresting of the Scriptures. Where they contradict his view, he boldly declares them to be metaphorical, as may be seen from a perusal of the remainder of the treatise from which we have quoted.

NOTE 19, p. 14.

Priestley, *History of the Corruptions of Christianity*, Part II. Introduction. He goes on to say (Section 1.) that "though the sacred writers often speak of the malignant nature of sin, they never go a single step farther and assert that 'it is of so heinous a nature that God cannot pardon it without an adequate satisfaction being made to His justice, and the honour of His laws and government.'" Whether the proposition he combats is *implicitly* contained in the Scripture utterances on the point may be disputed. It cannot be said that it is anywhere *explicitly* affirmed. But that Scripture anywhere explicitly affirms, as Priestley declares, the "contrary sentiment," namely, that "repentance and a good life are, *of themselves*, sufficient to recommend us to the Divine favour" (*ibid.*) is equally untrue. And it is remarkable that Priestley only attempts to cite the Old Testament in defence of this position, ignoring the fact that the New Testament is the Divine explanation of the principles upon which the Divine acceptance of repentance under the Old Covenant was founded. Dr. Priestley, however, in his exposition (Section III.) of the passages of Scripture relating to redemption, and the price paid for our sins, deals very liberally with figurative explanations. The Epistle to the Hebrews, which he dismisses as an "Epistle of an unknown author," without any reference to its undoubted antiquity (it is cited largely by the earliest of the Apostolic Fathers, Clemens Romanus), abounds, he says, "with the strongest figures, metaphors, and allegories." He goes on to remark that the Divinity of Christ is maintained on the ground that He should be able to make atonement for the "infinite evil" of the "smallest offence" committed against "an infinite Being," and declares the whole system to be "a disgrace to Christianity, which it must either throw off, or sink under."

NOTE 20, p. 14.

Carpenter, *Examination of the Charges made against Unitarians*, p. 155.

NOTE 21, p. 15.

Martineau, *Studies of Christianity*, Inconsistency of the Scheme of Vicarious Redemption, pp. 86, 87. Mr. Martineau rejects the doctrine of Vicarious Satisfaction, among other reasons, because there is nothing in nature and life at all analogous to it. "There is nowhere to be found," he proceeds, "any proper transfer or exchange, either of the qualities, or of the consequences, of vice and virtue" (p. 94). "The harmless" (p. 95) may "suffer by the guilty," but "there is no substitution; the distress of the offending party is not struck out of the offender's punishment; does not lessen, but rather aggravates his guilt." "Oh what deplorable reflection of human artifice is this," he exclaims (p. 97), "that Heaven is too veracious to abandon its menace against transgressors, yet is content to visit it on goodness the most perfect! No darker deed could be imagined than is thus ascribed to the Source of all perfection, under the insulted names of truth and holiness. What reliance could we have upon the faithfulness of such a Being? If it be consistent with His nature to punish by substitution, what security is there that He will not reward vicariously?" He disclaims against the inconsistency of declaring that the union of the Divine and human in Christ gave an infinite value to His sufferings, and at the same time teaching that it was in His Manhood alone that Christ suffered. He makes, however, a very valuable admission (p. 108): "Let me acknowledge that this statement concerning the moral effects of conscious pardon [involved in the ordinary teaching concerning the Atonement] is by no means an unmixed error. It touches upon a very profound and important truth; and I can never bring myself to regard that assurance of Divine forgiveness which the doctrine of Atonement imparts, as a demoralising state of mind encouraging laxity of conscience and a continuance in sin. The sense of pardon . . . binds the child of redemption, by all generous and filial obligations, to serve with free and willing heart the God who has gone forth to meet him." His explanation of the texts which speak of Christ's death as the price of our redemption is a peculiar one. He abandons the attempt of Priestley and Socinus to regard these statements as figurative. He regards them as relating to the introduction of the Gentiles to the privileges of the covenant, which until Christ's death had taken place was impossible (p. 112). It is not, however, quite clear why "as long as Christ remained on earth, He *necessarily* confined His ministry to His nation," nor why Christ's death "broke down the barriers of His Hebrew personality, and rendered Him spiritual as well as immortal" (p. 140). It is to be lamented that, in the face of the whole tenor of the Scriptures, he insists (p. 136, note) that "the Saviour offered up a sacrifice for His own sins, as well as for those of the people." But he comes very near the truth when he says (p. 141), "We have seen the Apostles justly announcing their Lord's death as a *proper propitiation*, because it placed whole classes of men, without any meritorious change in their character, in saving relations: declaring it a *strict substitute* for others' punishment, on the ground that there were those who must have perished, if He had not; and that He died and retired that they might remain alive: describing it as a *sacrifice that put away sin;* because it did that for ever, which the Levitical atonement did for a day: but we have not found them ever appealing to it either as a satisfaction to the justice of God, or an example of martyrdom to men."

NOTE 22, p. 16.

Greg, *Creed of Christendom*, p. 243. According to this earnest writer punishment is not inflicted capriciously, but follows guilt by a natural law, and redemption thus "becomes of necessity, not a saving but a regenerating process" [Catholic theology would say a saving, *because* a regenerating process]. He goes on, with strict accuracy, according to the teaching of Scripture and the Church Catholic, to say that "we can be redeemed from sin only by being redeemed from its commission." So we read in 1 John ii. 4, iii. 6, 9, v. 18, not to travel beyond one single Epistle. "Punishment," Mr. Greg continues, "being not the penalty, but the result of sin—being not an arbitrary and artificial annexation but an ordinary and logical consequence—cannot be borne by any one but the sinner." This statement is inaccurate. There is no one who does not in some degree suffer punishment for other men's sins. But with regard to Scripture teaching in reference to punishment, it is clear that Christ came to take away not merely punishment, but *sin itself.* See Matt. i. 21; Rom. viii. 1, 2, 4; Heb. ix. 26; 1 Pet. ii. 24; 1 John iii. 5.

Note 23, p. 16.

Archbishop Magee, whose views on the doctrine were evidently modified by his controversy with Priestley and his disciples, defines *expiatory* as that "in which by the suffering and death of the victim, the displeasure of God was averted from the person for whom it was offered, and the punishment due to his sins remitted, *whether the suffering of the victim was supposed to be strictly of a vicarious nature or not.*" Cudworth defines it as "the appointed means of preservation." See Magee, *Discourses and Dissertations*, No. 33.

In the *Theological Repository*, vol. i. p. 44, Priestley attempts to prove "that the pardon of sin is not, according to the Christian scheme, dispensed with any *particular* regard to the death or sufferings of Christ; as if they were, in the sense of divines, the PROCURING CAUSE of that blessing, and were NECESSARY in order *to remove some* IMPEDIMENT to the natural and essential placability of the Divine nature." See Archbishop Magee on the Atonement, who *does not hold* the view here controverted. It is described by Carpenter (*Examination of the Charges made against Unitarians*, p. 155), as "one of the mildest forms of the doctrine of satisfaction."

Priestley again says, "Hence has the ever-blessed God come to be considered as not naturally propitious to His offending creatures, and refusing His mercy to penitent offenders, till

His justice was satisfied with the death of His innocent Son; who is supposed to have sustained the utmost effects of the wrath of God, in the place of men, that by sin had exposed themselves to it." Priestley, *Theol. Rep.* I. p. 124.

Archbishop Magee has very cautious observations in reference to this phase of the controversy. Thus (*Discourses and Dissertations*, No. 17), he says, "That men *could* not have been forgiven unless Christ had suffered to purchase their forgiveness is no part of the doctrine of the Church of England. What God *could* or *could not* have done, it presumes not to pronounce." Again (*Discourses*, &c., No. 30), "Christ submitted Himself to suffering and death, that thereby *we* might be saved from undergoing the punishment of our transgressions. Will it not follow, that Christ's suffering stood in the place of ours, even though it might not be of the *same nature*, in any respect, with that which we were to have undergone?" Once more (*Discourses*, &c., No. 38, On the *Vicarious Import* of the Mosaic Sacrifices), "I have used the expression vicarious *import*, rather than *vicarious*, to avoid furnishing any colour to the idle charge made against the doctrine of Atonement, of supposing a real substitution in the room of the offender and a literal translation of his guilt and punishment to the immolated victim; a thing utterly incomprehensible, as neither *guilt* nor *punishment* can be conceived, but with reference to consciousness, which cannot be transferred. . . If it be asked, what connection can subsist between the death of the animal and the acquittal of the sinner, I answer without hesitation, I know not." He goes on to represent the offering of the animal as "vicarious *in symbol.*" Again, "no such notion as a strict vicarious substitution, or literal equivalent," belongs to the doctrine of Atonement, yet Archbishop Magee holds (*Discourses*, &c., No. 43) that Christ's Death is a proper sacrifice possessing "expiatory virtue" (No. 42) and producing effects "strictly propitiatory" (*ibid.*). It was (No. 73) "*more strictly vicarious* than the Mosaic sacrifices."

NOTE 24, p. 16.

Jowett, *Commentary on St. Paul.*

NOTE 25, p. 17.

Maurice, *Theological Essays*, 3rd Edition, pp. 146–148. Again, p. 148, "The tenacity with which my orthodox brethren have maintained notions at variance, as I think, with their inmost faith, has been owing in a great measure to their Unitarian opponents. They have heard the faith and the opinions assailed together; they have supposed that there must be an intimate connection between them; they have feared to ask whether there is or not."

Some orthodox divines, however, have not held themselves bound to make no distinction between faith and opinion on this subject, as the following extract from Veysie's *Bampton Lectures*, delivered in 1795, may serve to show. "It has indeed been usual to state the doctrine in a fuller manner, so as not simply to assert our reconciliation to God by the blood of Christ, but also to superadd the ground and reason of the reconciliation. And this addition, derived not so much from the positive declarations of Scripture, as from the views which men have entertained of the subject, and their reasonings respecting it, has been so generally acquiesced in and acknowledged, that it is commonly supposed . . . to be an essential part of the doctrine. But, however, here in itself it has unfortunately occasioned much misrepresentation and unjust censure, and (as we shall see in the sequel) has been the foundation of most of the principal objections against the doctrine itself." Veysie, *Bampton Lectures,* p. 15.

He proceeds to refer to the doctrine, "that Christ died to make satisfaction to the Divine justice," as one of the "adventitious circumstances with which the real question has been implicated:" so that "the doctrine of Satisfaction has been commonly used as a synonymous expression for the doctrine of Atonement" (p. 16). "For though it was anciently taken, in what is still its sole Scriptural sense, to signify reconciliation, yet because reconciliations are for the most part brought about by the aggressor's making satisfaction for his wrong by the payment of an equivalent to the party aggrieved, therefore in process of time atonement came to signify *compensation* and *satisfaction*" (p. 16). Veysie shows that the two doctrines of Atonement to which he refers are not justly liable to Priestley's strong condemnation, although not binding on orthodox theologians.

The present Archbishop of York speaks with similar reserve on the subject. He complains (*Bampton Lectures*, p. 178) that "the early writers exhibited a growing tendency to push the bounds of speculation beyond the lines of Scripture," and to enter upon questions which, though not "without interest to the mind of man," are such as "the Word of God, explicit as it is upon all points needful to be known for salvation, does not encourage us to pursue." Again, p. 181, he says that "the scheme is set forward with sufficient clearness for all practical purposes, but the theory has not been entirely unfolded." And this, he adds, is because, "having no parallel in human experience," the doctrine "cannot be made intelligible in a complete theory." From all which it may be seen how utterly unfair it is to charge the Church of England or, as is shown in Lect. III., the Church of Christ in general, with having laid down any theory of the satisfaction of God's justice or His wrath against sin, by the infliction of the punishment of death upon Jesus Christ.

LECTURE II.

Note 1, p. 20.

"From all which it is manifest that the Scriptural meaning of *atonement* is *reconciliation*, and accordingly to assert of Christ that He hath *made an atonement for us* by His blood, is the same as to assert that He hath reconciled us to God by His blood; or in other words, that by His death He hath made God propitious to sinful man, and hath procured to all who believe in Him pardon and acceptance.

"And this proposition contains, as I conceive, all that is essential to the doctrine of Atonement." Veysie, *Bampton Lectures*, p. 14.

Note 2, p. 20.

"A mind of piety may often be tempted to embrace hypotheses, and to arrive at conclusions because of their manifold usefulness in removing difficulties and illustrating the equity of God's government of the world. . . But a solid judgment and a cautious understanding should ever be on its guard against a delusion so soothing, and so inconsistent with the humility of a finite spirit." Benson, *Hulsean Lectures* for 1822, p. 200.

Note 3, p. 21.

See Ernst von Lasaulx. *Die Sühnopfer der Griechen und Römer und ihr Verhältniss zu dem Einen auf Golgotha.* Especially pp. 1, 5, 7.

Note 4, p. 21.

As Lasaulx puts it, "Prayer and sacrifice are the oldest and most common kind of Divine worship. Perhaps we might go so far as to say that the first word of primitive man would be a prayer, and his first act when fallen a sacrifice." *Ibid.* p. 1. But that the offering of sacrifice expressed other ideas than propitiation for sin is clear enough. It permeated the whole life of the ancients. Nothing was done without it. War, the administration of justice, marriage, birth, death, harvest, and an infinity of other things were consecrated by it. And from the earliest times it was regarded, not merely as an atonement for sin, but as an offering to win the Divine favour. Compare Rameses to Ammon (*Records of the Past*, vol. ii.). "Have not I made thee monuments very many? filled thy temple with spoils? built thee houses for millions of years? given treasures to thy house? enriched thy sacrifices with thirty thousand bulls, &c.?"

"The most ordinary conception of sacrifice was that of a presentation of something to God outside ourselves, whereby the inner presentation and sanctification of the spirit should receive completion." Tholuck, Beilage II. *On Epistle to the Hebrews*, p. 108.

Note 5, p. 24.

Benson, *Hulsean Lectures*, p. 240. His view of the institution of sacrifice accorded with this declaration. He says (p. 185), "It will be both wiser and safer to explain the phrase in which it is said that 'to Abel and his offering the Lord had, but to Cain and his offering He had not respect,' as referring to the individuals alone, or at least as comprehending both the individuals and their sacrifices." He rejects the idea that the lamb of Abel was slain "as an expiatory and propitiatory sacrifice, an express and intended prefiguration of the great Christian Atonement" (p. 186), on the ground that to suppose the "first parents of mankind" to have been "clearly informed with regard to the person, the office, and the sufferings of the Messiah . . . contradicts the whole tenor of Scripture." He admits that the Almighty *might* have commanded animal sacrifices as prefiguring the Sacrifice of Christ, but asks for any evidence whatever, beyond mere surmise or assumption, that He *did* do so. The question is, he reminds us (p. 200), not whether such an explanation of Abel's sacrifice is simple, but whether it is true. His view of the original institution of sacrifice is that "it was an offering of everything from which benefit was derived," "a most natural mode of expressing gratitude," "an innocent, a pious, an appropriate act of homage" (p. 241). Maurice, *Doctrine of Sacrifice*, p. 3, puts the matter most forcibly thus: "We are bound never to assume the existence of a *decree* which is not expressly announced to us." See also Browne, *Bampton Lectures* for 1806, p. 122.

Note 6, p. 24.

Butler, *Analogy*, Part II. ch. v.

Note 7, p. 25.

Bähr, *Symbolik des Mosaischen Cultus*, Book III. ch. I. sec. 4, thus classifies the various theories of sacrifice. The first idea is the *anthropopathic* one; that is, the theory which represents the offerer of sacrifice as picturing God to himself as like a human being, and offering to Him what he thought would please a human being. He points out that the blood is *not* eaten as food. The second or *juridical* theory, regards the sacrifice as a *vicarious substitution*. A third, which he calls the *physico-magnetic* theory, supposes a real and immediate influence (*einwirkung*) of the blood of the offering on (*auf*) the offerer. The fourth theory (that of Hasenkamp, which he does but epitomise in a phrase) regards the animal as for the moment representing the man,

He cites against the first of these theories a dialogue from an ancient Hindoo source in which the inquirer asks whether God eats and drinks as man. The answer is, "God does not eat and drink like a mortal man. If you do not love Him, your offering will not be worthy in His sight. For since all mankind enjoy freely the good things of this world (für sich begehren), God, on His part, requires of them a free-will offering of their substance as the strongest evidence of their thankfulness and affection."

A somewhat different list will be found in Tholuck on the Epistle to the Hebrews (*Beilage* II. p. 75). The most remarkable of the theories he mentions is a form of Bähr's third theory, namely, that the blood, being the sensual principle, may be regarded also as the principle of sin, and that the offering up of this to God is a physical expiation for sin.

As regards the threefold view of Sacrifice presented by the Jewish Law, the language used in the lecture perhaps requires further explanation. The first class had in view propitiation for sin, the second the public recognition of God whether by praise or prayer, and the third the consecration of the life of the worshipper.

Note 8, p. 25.

The whole question will be found discussed at full length in Kurz's *Sacrificial Worship of the Old Testament*, pp. 92 sqq. After a long argument as to whether the victim were the real *alter ego* or the ideal *ipse ego* of the worshipper, he inclines to the former. I am constrained to come to a different conclusion. Bähr (*Symbolik* II. 211) regards the victim as a *substitute* for the worshipper. Yet this substitution, he adds, "is no formal (förmliche) interchange of parts, no external or real, but a symbolic substitution, so that *if that which it ought to represent did not exist on the part of the offerer, it became empty and vain.*" To this *symbolic* substitution the laying on of hands seems to me to point. The character of the offerer is symbolically transferred to the victim, and the whole rite is a representation in type and symbol of the proper attitude of the soul to God.

NOTE 9, p. 25.

Kurz discusses this subject at full length. I have not been able to accept, without qualification, any one of the various theories he discusses.

NOTE 10, p. 26.

See authorities in Kurz's *Sacrificial Worship of the Old Testament*, pp. 189–213. "There is," he says, "scarcely a single question connected with the whole range of biblical theology on which there has been so much pure conjecture, and about the settlement of which theological science was so late in arriving at a correct conclusion." It was obviously impossible to enter upon so vast a subject in these lectures themselves. But it may be here remarked that the conclusion arrived at in the lecture gives only one side of the question. In a broader and deeper view still *every* transgression, even committed in ignorance, involves human corruption, and hence moral guilt. And thus, after all the distinctions, the Law of Moses comes back to the fact that sin (חטאת) and trespass (אשם) are virtually the same. Lev. v. 6–13, 17–19. In this last passage "is he guilty" is literally "he hath *trespassed*" (אשם), and it is so rendered in v. 18. See also Lev. vi. 25, 26. The rules for some of the sin offerings seem to have been somewhat indefinite, as may be seen by comparing the last cited passage with Lev. iv. 22–35. The real truth seems to have been that, in its widest sense, the word חטאת included both voluntary and involuntary transgression.

NOTE 11, p. 27.

The root of the word אשם seems to imply indifference, carelessness, neglect. See Gesenius, *Thes.* s. v.

NOTE 12, p. 27.

See authorities in Kurz. The best part of the victim becomes the priest's. The proper translation of שׁוֹק would appear to be *leg*, and not *shoulder*, as in our version. So Gesenius admits, when he declares its original meaning to be "pars pedis a genu ad talum."

NOTE 13, p. 29.

The word *Azazel* (A. V., scape-goat) has been variously explained. Gesenius compares it with a cognate word used by the Arabs for an evil demon. But this was probably a word of later origin. Tholuck (*Beilage* II. on Ep. to Hebrews, p. 80) seems to have hit on the right idea when he explains it as the Pe'alpal from עֲזֵל as חֲצוֹצֵר for חֲצַרְצַר (Gesenius, however, has abandoned this last derivation for חֲצוֹצְרָה, *trumpet*). In this case it would be a strong intensive form from a word signifying "separation;"—the separated, the abandoned one. The Revised Version explains by "dismissal."

NOTE 14, p. 30.

Much unnecessary ingenuity has been expended upon the endeavour to discover *which* lamb it is to which the Baptist makes reference, when in John i. 25 he calls Jesus "the Lamb of God, that taketh away (or *beareth*) the sins of the world." It might have been supposed possible for so great and awful a sacrifice to have combined, at least to some extent, the characteristics of *all* the Jewish sacrifices.

NOTE 15, p. 30.

There are three words used in the Old Testament to express the idea of propitiation. The first, כָּפַר, is rendered *atonement* in 75 passages of Scripture. The Piel (כִּפֶּר) is rendered *reconcile, make reconciliation* in Lev. vi. 30 (23 in Heb.), viii. 15, as also in

Ezek. xlv. 15, 17, Dan. ix. 24. It is rendered "purge away" or "purge" in eight places, "forgive" in two, "pacify" in two, and in Isa. xxviii. 18 it is used (in the Pual) of a covenant which is disannulled, in Numb. xxxv. 33 of a land which cannot be cleansed from her iniquities, and in Gen. xxxii. 20 (Heb. 21) of appeasing Esau's wrath with a present. The second (נשא) is never directly translated *atonement*, but is closely connected with it in passages like Lev. x. 17, where it means to bear the iniquity of the congregation, cf. Exod. xxviii. 29, 30, 38. The third, סלח, is translated indifferently "pardon" or "forgive," and in one place (Deut. xxix. 20—in Heb. 19) "spare."

With regard to the doctrine that the life-principle is in the blood, see Archbishop Thompson's *Bampton Lectures*, Lect. II., and especially note 28, for evidence that ancients and moderns regarded the blood as the seat of that principle. The Archbishop refers to the *taurobolion*, a heathen custom mentioned by Prudentius, in which it was the practice to allow the blood of the slaughtered animal to flow freely over the offerer, after which he regarded himself as "regenerated for ever" (in aeternum renatus). Philo repeatedly refers to Lev. xvii. 11. See his *Deterius Potiori Insidiatur*. (Works II. 206 ed. Mangey) in which he says that the blood is the substance (οὐσία) of the life (ψυχή), and his *Quis Rerum Divinarum Haeres*, Works II. 480. Again, he regards the shedding of blood as the effusion of the life; ψυχῆς γὰρ, κυρίως εἰπεῖν, ἐστὶ σπονδὴ τὸ αἷμα. *De Animalibus Sacrificio Idoneis. Ibid.* I. 242, 10.

NOTE 16, p. 31.

The word λύτρον, derived from λύω, is literally *that which looses*, hence the price paid for the redemption of a captive (so Cremer's *Lexicon*). But when he goes on to say that "the ransom price is an expiation or (Numb. xxxv. 13) an equivalent for the *punishment* due, and therefore frees from the *consequences* of guilt," he is on less safe ground. For surely what is due from man is *obedience*, not the endurance of punishment. And that from which man is freed is guilt itself, not its consequences alone. The price paid, then, is obedience to the law of God. In 1 Tim. ii. 6 Christ is Himself the ἀντίλυτρον or price of redemption paid ὑπέρ, on behalf of, all. Therefore here, clearly it is not the *punishment* or *sufferings* of Christ which are that price. ἀντίλυτρον is properly (see Stephens' *Thesaurus* s.v.) an *exchange* of captives or the like. Bretschneider compares the ἀντίψυχον of 3 Macc. vi. 29, xvii. 22. But Ignatius uses this expression of himself, in his Epistle to the Ephesians ch. xxi., in that to the Smyrnaeans, ch. x., and in that to Polycarp, ch. ii., and vi. He could not have meant that his death was the vicarious death of a substitute on behalf of their sins, but simply that he hoped that by *his* death *they* might profit. Hefele explains his meaning by "ego vicissim recreo." The phrase was often used by Athanasius, Eusebius, Gregory of Nazianzus and others. But it clearly involves the offer of a *life for a life*.

Note 17, p. 31.

Where ὑπέρ has, as it occasionally has, the sense of "instead of," it seems usually to mean "in the name" or "authority of." So that the idea of substitution would seem never to be necessarily implied in it.

Note 18, p. 32.

It is worthy of remark that the new covenant established between God and His people through Jesus Christ is not said to be ratified by His Death but by His Blood. The significance of this will appear by a reference to Lev. xvii. 11, above cited. See St. Luke xxii. 20, 1 Cor. x. 16. Heb. ix. 15-18 is discussed in the lecture. The use of προσφορά and θυσία in reference to the Death of Christ, which is frequent in the Epistle to the Hebrews, proves nothing either way until we have decided in what the efficacy of the offering or sacrifice consisted, whether it was the death of the victim, considered as punishment, or its life, considered as spotless, and therefore well pleasing to God.

Note 19, p. 33.

Though the balance of authority is against it, the translation "covenant" here appears to give the best sense. Meyer, Alford, Moll (in Lange's *Commentary*), and lately Farrar, may be cited in favour of the rendering "testament;" Grotius, Michaelis, Tholuck and Ebrard in favour of "covenant." The latter asks whether it is true that a testament cannot exist without the death of the testator, and contends that instead of "is" we should have had "is acted upon" or "is opened." He also urges that if διαθήκη mean testament, then, in reference to the Old Testament, God who is the "testator" is represented as necessarily dead. To this we may add that God, not Christ as Mediator, is equally the testator in the New Testament, if we accept this rendering. But since διατίθεμαι frequently means to arrange, establish, διαθέμενος may mean he who effects such a covenant, the mediator between the two parties. This in the Old Covenant was ritually and figuratively the slain victim, in the New it was Jesus Christ. This view, it must be admitted, derives some force from the context, beside avoiding the extraordinary change of meaning in the most important word in the passage, without a word of warning or explanation on the author's part. Let us examine that context, and see what, on this view, the connexion of thought is. The sacred writer is pointing out the transitory nature of the Old Covenant. The ritual of the law, he says, prefigured the truth that the way into the holiest was not yet manifest, the gifts and sacrifices being of a kind only to typify, and not actually to effect the cleansing of the worshipper. Christ, however, when He came, entered into the only really holy place, namely, heaven, having by His own Blood obtained eternal redemption for us. If it be true that there was some virtue in the sacrifices under the law, how much more was this the case with the Sacrifice of Christ, of which the sacrifices of the law were types? This is why He is the Mediator of a New Covenant, and why His Death was a necessary part of His mediatorial work. For wherever there is a covenant, there of necessity is the death of that (or Him, *i.e.* the victim) which ratifies it. For a covenant is invariably ratified by the death of sacrificed victims,* nor do we ever find it ratified while the ratifier is alive. And this is the reason why the first covenant was not dedicated without blood. Moses slew the victims and sprinkled the book and all the people, saying, This is the blood of the covenant which God hath commanded you. Thus the principle is laid down that without shedding of blood there is no remission. This truth was shadowed forth in the ceremonial of the law; it was witnessed to by the practice of almost all nations from the first; but it was actually manifested in the Death and Ascension of Jesus Christ. With regard to $διαθέμενος$ in the sense of the maker of a covenant, we have only to compare Acts iii. 25, where it will certainly not be argued that God was dead, and that the law was the testament He left behind Him. Here, however, the mediator, He by whose shedding of blood the covenant is confirmed, is said to make the covenant. See Aristoph. *Birds* 440, 1. $διατίθεμαι$ also means to compose a quarrel, which gives the sense of "mediator" to $διαθέμενος$. See Xenoph. *Memorab.* II. 6. 23. This discussion is not altogether beside the purpose of these lectures, if it brings out from the passage discussed that the principle had always been recognised that the offer of an innocent life alone could make reconciliation between God and man.

* See Latin "icere foedus."

Note 20, p. 34.

It has the first meaning in Mark v. 35, ix. 26, Luke viii. 53, John vi. 49, 58 (where, however, the other rendering is admissible), viii. 53, xi. 15, &c. The last is found in Matt. viii. 32, Luke xvi. 22, xx. 29, 32, &c. St. Paul's use, however, is strongly in favour of the latter rendering. See also p. 128.

Note 21, p. 37.

The word ίλασμός strictly signifies the propitiatory process, "actio qua laesus et offensus placatur" (Schleusner). Hence (as Cremer in his Lexicon) it comes to mean Christ in Whom the person and work are one. Christ, in fact, is identified with His work. In the LXX. either it or its compound ἐξιλασμός is used as the equivalent of the Hebrew *caphar* (cover) in Lev. xxiii. 27, 28, xxv. 9, Numb. v. 8, &c., and more exactly as the equivalent of *salach* (to make pleased) in Ps. cxxix. (A. V. cxxx.) 4, Dan. ix. 9. In Ezek. xliv. 27 it translates חטאת (sin-offering) and in Amos viii. 14 it appears as the translation of אשמה (trespass-offering). We may compare the use of ίλάσθητι "be pacified" in Luke xviii. 13. The word ίλαστήριον, following as it does the analogy of words like δικαστήριον, θυσιαστήριον, and the like, signifies the *place where* propitiation is made. This word in the LXX. appears as the translation of mercy-seat, save in four places in the Old Testament. In one of these, Amos ix. 1, the LXX. translators have read mercy-seat (*capporeth*) for *caphtor*, by a transposition of the letters. The other three passages occur in Ezek. xliii. 14, 17, 20, where it wrongly translates the Hebrew word *'azarah*. This is clear (1) from the fact that the same word is translated by ἱερόν in ch. xlv. 19, and (2) from the fact that the Vulgate translates it by *crepido*, a ledge, border, or basement. The mercy-seat (see Exod. xxv. 22, Lev. xvi. 2, 14, 15) is the place where the blood (or life) of the victim meets the presence and glory of God. No fitter term could be employed to designate Him Who in His Death rendered up His human soul unto Himself.

NOTE 22, p. 38.

A literal translation of the passage may serve to make its scope clearer. Sometimes in a translation meanings are imported into a passage which exist only in the mind of the translator. The literal translation of vv. 4–7 is as follows:— *Surely our diseases* (or griefs) *He hath borne* (or taken away— the word has both senses), *and our sorrows, He hath borne them, but as for us, we looked on Him as one stricken, smitten of God, and afflicted. But He was pierced* (or made to suffer) *by our offences, He was crushed* (or bruised) *by our iniquities, the chastisement* (the word signifies *disciplinary* punishment) *of our peace was on Him, and with His stripes healing was imparted to us. All we like sheep had gone astray, we had turned every one to his own way, and the Lord hath caused to fall* (or light) *on Him the iniquity of us all.*

It may be observed that though the particle translated "for" in the A.V. in the passage "He was wounded for our offences" has sometimes that meaning, it has far more often the meaning "by," and still more often the sense of "from," in the sense of the cause. Thus the passage would mean "our offences were the cause of His being wounded," but not necessarily that He was wounded instead of us for our offences. The whole point of the argument lies in this, Did Christ suffer in order to remove suffering and its cause, sin, from us, or merely to avert the Father's wrath from us? May we content ourselves with saying that our offences brought affliction on Christ, or are we bound to go further, and say that He suffered in our stead precisely what we had deserved to endure?

NOTE 23, p. 43.

Mr. Herbert Spencer has repeated the statement that Christianity rests upon the principle of vicarious substitution once more in the *Nineteenth Century* for the month in which these lectures were delivered. Surely it is time that the religion of Christ were held responsible solely for what it teaches, and not for what men have taken upon themselves to teach in its name.

LECTURE III.

Note 1, p. 45.

Clement, First Epistle to the Corinthians, ch. vii. It has "brought in," he says, "the grace of repentance to the whole world." The words "grace of repentance" must not be read in the light of mediæval glosses. The "grace of repentance" is that gift of God's loving-kindness which enables us to effect in ourselves a change of heart and purpose (μετανοία). So the scarlet thread hung by Rahab from her house is typical of the "redemption" which should take place "through the Blood of the Lord to all who believe and hope in God." *Ib.* ch. xii. So in ch. xvi. he translates Isa. liii. 10 by "the Lord hath given Him up for our sins."

Note 2, p. 45.

Barnabas, Epistle, ch. vii. He also (ch. v.) refers to the death of Christ as intended "to abolish death," to Christ as enduring it in order to bring to a head the wickedness of mankind. The scape-goat is regarded as a type of Christ accursed for our sins (ch. vii.). The red heifer (ch. viii.) and the brazen serpent (ch. xii.) are also a type of Christ, the latter only because "it behoved Him to suffer and to quicken." The text is here probably deficient, and we should probably supply words such as "those who believe in Him." And in ch. ii. he says that the law was abolished in order that the new law of our Lord Jesus Christ, which is without the yoke of necessity, should have a human victim.

Note 3, p. 45.

Epistle to Trallians, ch. 8, and Epistle to the Romans, ch. 7.

The Epistle to Diognetus has been regarded by many persons as spurious. The last attack upon it is to be found in the *Church Quarterly Review* for April 1877. The attack does not, however, manifest much of the true critical faculty. It consists chiefly in citing a number of passages usually regarded as quotations from this Epistle by other authors, and building on them the theory that the Epistle was fabricated out of these passages of the Fathers by Stephens in the sixteenth century, that being an era in which many such fabrications were made. But the theory requires that Stephens should not only have been a very skilful forger, but that he should have taken immense care and pains to exclude all passages of the Fathers which breathed any spirit but that of the first century and a half of the Christian era. The errors combated in the Epistle are of a very early date. And it is most remarkable that the language held in reference to the Sacrifice of Christ displays not a trace of the theory so common among the Fathers, which originated with Irenæus at a date subsequent to that to which this Epistle is commonly assigned, which regards the price paid by Christ as paid to the devil. The passage referring to the Atonement is not only one of singular beauty, but one which altogether steers clear of the later theories which have surrounded the doctrine of Atonement with so many difficulties. It runs as follows :—

"But when the measure of our wickedness was filled up, and it was plainly manifested that its reward, chastisement and death, was hanging over us, and when the time came in which God had purposed to manifest for the future His kindness and power as though by the operation of one love of surpassing tenderness toward men, He hated us not, neither did He spurn us, neither was He mindful of our iniquities; but He was long-suffering, He bore with us, and as He Himself saith, He took on Him our sins; He Himself gave His own Son a ransom for us; the holy for the transgressors, the blameless for the wicked, the just for the unjust, the incorruptible for the corruptible, the immortal for the mortal. For what else could cover our sins but His Righteousness? In whom could we, the transgressors and ungodly, be justified, except in the Son of God alone? O sweet exchange! O unsearchable process! O benefits most unexpected! that the transgression of many should be hid in one Just One, and the righteousness of One should justify many transgressors. Epistle to Diognetus, ch. ix.

NOTE 4, p. 46.

In a fragment preserved in Leontius against the Eutychians. Justin Martyr's writings, though much more voluminous than those which have already passed under review, contain singularly few allusions to the doctrine of reconciliation by the Sacrifice of Christ. Most of his allusions are brief, and do not extend beyond the doctrine of Scripture. But in the Dialogue with Trypho the Jew, ch. xciv.-xcvi. he denies emphatically that Jesus was cursed of God because He hung on the Cross, yet asserts that Jesus Christ took on Him the curses of all, and suffered on behalf of the whole family of mankind. He again asserts (ch. cxxxviii.) that we are regenerated and saved from God's impending judgment "by water, faith and *wood*" (διὰ ξύλου, the expression frequently used in the Scriptures of the Cross).

NOTE 5, p. 46:

Irenæus, *Against Heresies*, Book v. Ch. i.

NOTE 6, p. 46.

In his Homily on St. Matthew, tom. xvi., Origen asks the question, "To whom did Christ give His soul a ransom for many?" and answers it, though not so decidedly as some would have us believe, "for if it was not to God, was it not to the evil one, for he had us in his power until the soul ($\psi\upsilon\chi\acute{\eta}$) of Jesus was given to him as the ransom for sin?" This suggestion of Origen's is read into other passages (as by Redepenning, *Origenes* II. 405-7). It may however be found elsewhere in his writings, as in his Exposition of Rom. iv. 11. The idea evidently was that Christ manifested His own and His Father's love by giving Himself for us into the power of the devil to do his utmost with. The devil deceived himself when he proceeded to wreak his vengeance upon Jesus. But it is not very clear from Origen how this giving Himself up to the power of the devil made atonement for sin. See Baur, *Die Christliche Lehre von der Versöhnung* (ed. 1838), p. 60. Baur shows from the Commentary on Rom. iii. 7, 8, that Origen distinguishes between redemption and remission of sins. Redemption is a price paid to an enemy. But the offering of Christ's Body was also a propitiation to God.* A different theory is advanced in Origen's treatise against Celsus, Book I. ch. xxxi. Here he seems to enter more into the mysterious nature of the question, and contends that it is probable in the nature of things that there may be a kind of mysterious virtue in the death of a righteous man for the common good. In his twenty-eighth Homily on St. John, ch. 14, he says, "But for the people died this man, a Being ($\zeta\tilde{\omega}o\nu$) purer than all beings, Who took away ($\tilde{\eta}\rho\epsilon$) our sins and our weaknesses, since He was able to take on Himself and to do away ($\lambda\tilde{\upsilon}\sigma\alpha\iota$) the sin of the whole world and to swallow it up and cause it to vanish, since He did no sin, neither was guile found in His mouth." And that Origen did not regard any one explanation as exhausting the mystery of the passion we learn from his sixth Homily on the same Gospel, ch. 37, where in commenting on the words "Behold the Lamb of God, that taketh away the sins of the world" he says, "And there is more than one way by which the Lamb Who

* See Notes 16 and 21 below.

taketh away the sins of the world, and commences His task by the slaying of Himself, can accomplish this work, and some of these are clear to the mass of mankind, but others unknown to so great a number, and known only to those who in God's Providence are thought fit for such knowledge." See also his Exposition of 2 Cor. v. 21, in the *Hom. in Joan.*, tom. 28. The student may also refer to Hagenbach's *History of Doctrines*, bearing in mind, however, that it has been the practice to represent Origen as definitely teaching the doctrine mentioned above. The truth is, as we have just seen, that it is but one suggestion among many others, thrown out towards the explanation of a mystery transcending our human reason.

Note 7, p. 46.

Greg. Nyss. *Orat. Catech.* ch. 23–26, and *Contr. Eunom.* Migne 890. The price paid, he says, was higher and greater than the thing bought (ch. 23), and he goes on to discuss (ch. 26) the justice of deceiving Satan, and establishes its fairness on the ground that it is the deceiver who is deceived. Basil is sometimes quoted as holding this view. But in his Commentary on Ps. xlviii. 7, 8, he appears rather to avoid this doctrine and to represent Christ as a propitiation ($ἐξίλασμα$) to God. Like other Fathers, however, he declares the price to be of more value than that which was bought by it.

Note 8, p. 46.

Servata est ergo in utroque peccato justitia Dei punientis. Nam et illum appensum est aequitatis examine, ut nec ipsius diaboli potestati negaretur homo, quem sibi male suadendo subjecerat. Iniquum enim erat ut ei quam ceperat, non dominaretur. . . Atque Verbum Dei, unicus Dei filius, diabolum. . . nihil ei extorquens violento dominatu sed superans eum lege justitiae. . . Justissime itaque dimittere cogitur credentes in eum quam injustissime occidit. *De Libero Arbitrio* III. 10.

NOTE 9, p. 47.

Leo the Great, *Serm.* XXII. 4, Illusa est seculi hostis astutia, qui nativitatem pueri in salutem generis humani procreati non aliter sibi quam omnium nascentium putaret obnoxiam. And Gregory the Great (*Moral.* in caput XL.; Job xxxiii. 7) Assumpsit enim corpus ut in eo Behemoth (Gregory expounds Behemoth to mean Satan) iste quasi escam suam mortem carnis appeteret. Quam mortem dum in illo injuste appetit, nos quos quasi juste tenebat amisit. So teaches St. John of Damascus, in the Greek Church. Augustin himself, however, does not appear to have put forward very explicitly the doctrine that Satan deceived himself.

NOTE 10, p. 47.

Baur correctly remarks that the views of the Fathers who did not accept the theory of a price paid to the devil were "indefinite and undeveloped" (*Die Christliche Lehre von der Versöhnung*, 1st period, sec. 2). In other words they accepted the *fact* of redemption without being prepared with a theory. The passages from Athanasius which contain his doctrine may be found in his treatise *De Incarnatione Verbi*, ch. 7, 8, 9, 20. The doctrine laid down in that treatise may be thus summarised. God had laid down in the law the principle, "the soul that sinneth, it shall die." If the sinner did *not* die, that principle would have been enunciated in vain. Yet it would not have been to His glory that His work should perish. What then was He to do? Was He to demand repentance ($μετάνοια$) from man? It were impossible, for He had decreed that to be holden in death ($κρατουμένων$ $ἐν$ $τῷ$ $θανάτῳ$) was the penalty man was to pay for sin. Nothing therefore remained but the intervention of the Divine Word, by Whom all things were made. "It was His task to bring forth again that which was corrupt into incorruption." "Seeing us all liable to death . . . He took a body and that not unlike ($ἀλλότριον$) to ours." "And thus, when He had taken from what was ours [a body] similar [to our own], since we were all liable to the corruption of death, and when He had delivered it up to death instead (ἀντί) of all, He presented (προσῆγε) it to the Father, doing this also in a spirit of love to man (φιλανθρώπως), in order, first, that inasmuch 'as all men died in Him,' the law concerning the corruption of mankind * (κατὰ τῆς φθορᾶς τῶν ἀνθρώπων) might be destroyed, since its power was fulfilled in the Body of the Lord, and it had no longer any place against mankind when they had become like to Him; and next, that He might bring back to incorruption the men whom He had restored from corruption, and might make them alive again from death, by His identification of Himself with the body, and by the grace of His Resurrection entirely removing death from them." *De Inc. Verbi*, ch. 8. So, in ch. 9, he says ἀντὶ πάντων ἱκανὸν γένηται τῷ θανάτῳ, and again adds "that corruption might cease from mankind by the grace of His Resurrection." He then proceeds to say that the Divine Word presenting (προσάγων) His own temple and bodily organ as an ἀντίψυχον for all, fulfilled all that was owing in death, and that being thus united by likeness (*i.e.*, by assuming our mortal body) to all of us, He, as was reasonable (εἰκότως), indued all with immortality in the promise concerning His Resurrection. Similarly c. 20. Three things may be noted here, (1) that there is a marked difference between the language of Athanasius and that of modern writers, (2) that the virtue of the Death of Christ is never severed from that of his Resurrection, and (3) that the ἀντίψυχον of which he speaks is just as likely to be the offering of the pure and sinless body of our Lord to God in the place of our defiled and corrupt bodies, as the endurance of a certain amount of bodily suffering in our stead. So St. Cyril teaches in the passage cited in p. 49. What He offers in our stead is there supposed to be, not the endurance of a certain number of pains and penalties, *but our righteousness*. For the passage in Irenæus see his Treatise against Heresies, v. 16.

* Observe how Athanasius explains 2 Cor. v. 14.

Note 11, p. 48.

Gregor. Nazianz. *Orations*, xxxiii. 9, and xlv. 22. In the former of these passages he speaks of us as not only saved, but *formed afresh* by the sufferings of Christ.

Note 12, p. 48.

See St. Chrysostom on 2 Cor. v. 21 and Gal. iii. 13.

Note 13, p. 49.

In his treatise against Nestorius, tom. v. See also his Commentary on Rom. iii. 21. He regarded the body of Christ as incapable of (permanent) death by reason of its union with the Word though it might "taste death." In his *Quod unus sit Christus*, Cyril approaches the mediæval theory of an equivalent ($\dot{a}\nu\tau\acute{a}\xi\iota\sigma\varsigma$). But his equivalent is one whose worthiness, not whose punishment, is accepted instead of ours. Cyril of Jerusalem puts this doctrine into another form. Christ is *more* than an equivalent. We have not committed so much sin as He has worked righteousness. (*Catechetical Lectures*, xiii. 33.)

Note 14, p. 50.

These statements will be found in pt. I., ch. xi. 2, 6, xiii. 7 and xiv. and in pt. II. ch. vi. St. Anselm's method is in many respects rationalism pure and simple. And some of his notions are very remarkable. Thus he contends that man was created in order to take the place of the angels who had fallen, an idea which he has obtained from St. Augustin's *Enchiridion ad Laurentium*, c. 29. See also that Father's *De Civitate Dei* xxii. The distinction between Anselm's view and that of more modern times appears to be this, that he did not teach that the *wrath* of God was satisfied by the *sufferings* of Jesus, nor that His sufferings were endured simply that we might not suffer.

I

NOTES TO LECTURE III.

NOTE 15, p. 50.

Abelard contends strongly against the notion that the devil had acquired a right over us by our sin. What right, he asks in his Commentary on the Epistle to the Romans, ch. 3, does a slave obtain over the fellow-slave whom he has tempted to transgress against his lord? And again, the devil deceived Adam and Eve, by promising immortality, which it was not in his power to give. He explains "set forth as a propitiation" by styling Christ our reconciler (reconciliator), and the process as consisting (1) in the manifestation of God's love to us, and (2) in the disposing us to love Him Who has done so great things for us. And again, Redemptio itaque nostra est illa summa in nobis per passionem Christi dilectio, quae nos [non?] solum a servitute peccati liberat, sed veram nobis filiorum Dei libertatem acquirit: ut amore ejus potius quam timore cuncta impleamus, qui nobis tantam exhibuit gratiam, qua major inveniri ipso attestante non potest. Works, pp. 549–553 (Paris ed. 1616).

Aquinas' views may be summed up as follows:—1. Christ died voluntarily. 2. His death was an act of obedience in order (*a*) to the justification of man, (*b*) to his reconciliation with God. 3. He satisfied God, Who was offended, by offering Him what He loved more than He hated the offence. The sacrifice of Christ therefore was more than sufficient, it was superabundant. 4. A sacrifice is a recognition of God's honour, and therefore propitiatory. 5. Man was (*a*) in bondage to sin and the devil, (*b*) liable to punishment for sin. Christ's Death and Passion was a superabundant satisfaction for both, a price paid which sets us free from either obligation. 6. For redemption one needs (*a*) the act of payment, (*b*) the price paid. 7. The Passion of Christ is the cause of remission of sins, (*a*) because it provokes us to charity, (*b*) because the Head redeems the members of His Body, (*c*) because the Flesh was the instrument of the Divinity. 8. It is the cause of our reconciliation to God, (*a*) because sin is removed by it, (*b*) because it was a sacrifice well-pleasing to God. 9. It behoved Christ to die, (*a*) to make satisfaction for mankind, condemned to death for sin, (*b*) to manifest His true manhood.

He deals very fully with the Sacrifice of Christ in his *Summa Theologiae*, Part III., Question 48. A brief sketch of his reasoning may be interesting. He asks first whether Christ's Passion was the cause of our salvation by means of His merit, and decides that it was (1) because His Passion was voluntary, (2) because He suffered to remove certain impediments in the way of our salvation, and (3) that a special merit attached to His Passion, not because it was a greater display of love, but because His death on the Cross was a suitable means of obtaining our pardon (see Quest. 46, Arts. 3 and 4). Next he asks whether Christ caused our salvation by the means of satisfaction. This he decides in the affirmative, (1) because the Head is one person mystically with the members, (2) because Christ's love in His Passion was greater than the malice of His enemies, and (3) because the dignity of His Flesh was infinite, by reason of its hypostatic union with the Godhead. His next inquiry is whether Christ's death caused our salvation as a sacrifice. He replies Yes, (1) because human and mortal flesh was the most suitable sacrifice that could be offered, (2) because it is a sign to us of truths expressed by it, (3) that though the death of Christ was no sacrifice on the part of those who slew Him, He made thus by His own will a sacrifice of Himself. The next question is, was His Passion a redemption? In this he rejects St. Augustine's view, and declares (1) that justice required that man should be redeemed in respect of God, not of the devil, and (2) that the price was paid, not to the devil but to God. Next he argues that Christ could properly be called our Redeemer, and lastly, that Christ effected our salvation as the efficient cause. Here he dwells on the spiritual efficacy of Christ's sacrifice by virtue of His Divinity, and sums up by saying that the *efficacy* of Christ's sacrifice was due to His being Divine, its *merit*, to the fact that it was a voluntary offering, its *satisfaction*, in that it was an offering of His Flesh, whereby we are freed from liability to punishment, its *redemption*, in what we are redeemed from the slavery of guilt, its *sacrifice*, because by it we are reconciled to God. It will thus be seen that Aquinas by no means explains the doctrine of our reconciliation by the Passion of Christ as a simple, but rather as an extremely complex, process. The Scotists, as against Aquinas, taught that Christ's sacrifice was not sufficient, but that by a process similar to one known to the Roman law as *acceptilatio*, it was regarded as though it were so. See Abp. Thomson's *Bampton Lectures*, Lect. V. p. 135. See also a digest of the views of Aquinas and Scotus in Ritschl's *Critical History of the Christian Doctrine of Justification and Reconciliation*, pp. 51–68.

NOTE 16, p. 51.

Luther, *Commentary on the Epistle to the Galatians*, ch. ii., iii. Sic mortuus est ut nos essemus vita in illo; sic confusus ut nos fieremus gloria, omnia pro nobis factus, ut omnia fieremus in illo, &c. He also contends that Christ must be considered as accursed by God because it is written "Cursed is every one that hangeth on a tree." The passage from Calvin is to be found in his *Institutes* II. xvi. 11. This view is not open to the objections which are raised against the theory of substitution pure and simple. For anger is not essentially incompatible with love. The anger of a parent is very often a sign of love, not of its absence. It is a question, too, whether God's wrath against sin can fairly be described from all points of view, as infinite. Beneath the abyss of that wrath there lies a yet deeper abyss of love. The "signs" of God's wrath and punishment Jesus Christ must bear, inasmuch as He has taken upon Himself to represent man. His doing so was but the confession of the justice of God's sentence against sinners. Yet in this God exacted no satisfaction of His vengeance against them.

Rather the fact that the Beloved Son of God endured those sufferings was a proof that God loved sinners, and that He designed to rescue them from the consequences their misdeeds had brought on them. It may be remarked that Francis Turretin, a theologian of high repute among the Calvinists, says (*Instit.* locus decimus quartus, quaestio xiii. sec. xii.) "satisfactio [Christi] *non externae tantum sanguinis oblationi* adscribenda est, *sed praecipue actui interno,* nimirum spontaneae ejus et constantissimae voluntati, qua sanctificari dicimur." The Reforming Divines gradually systematised this side, as well as the other, of Christ's atoning work. His passive obedience satisfied God's justice; His active obedience justified us, by bringing us into fellowship with His Holiness. See *Formula Concordiae,* Art. III. De fidei justitia coram Deo. "Eam ob causam ipsius obedientia (non ea tantum qua patri paruit in tota sua passione et morte, verum etiam qua nostra causa sponte se legi subjecit, eamque obedientia illa sua implevit) nobis ad justitiam imputatur." Baxter, *Aphorisms of Justification,* p. 30 (ed. 1655) speaks of this active and passive obedience of Christ as "a very great dispute among Divines." It was an advance when he came to see (*On the Imputation of Christ's Righteousness,* published in 1675) that "the ends of the law may be attained by the immediate merit of perfection as well as by suffering, but best by both."

NOTE 17, p. 53.

Further illustrations of the doctrine of the Reformed Churches may be found in the Saxon Confession, signed (among others) by Melanchthon, Bugenhagen and Alexander Hales, and in the Heidelberg Confession. The first asserts that "tanta est justitiae severitas, ut *non sit facta reconciliatio nisi poena persolveretur.* Tanta est irae magnitudo, ut aeternus Pater non sit placatus nisi deprecatione et morte Filii." This confession was presented at the Council of Trent, A.D.

1551. The latter declares that in His whole life on earth, but chiefly in His death (ejus extremo), He bore in body and soul *the anger of God* against the sin of the whole human race. It will be observed that this is what Calvin (as afterwards Jonathan Edwards, see p. 9) denies. The Basel Conference, in its fourth article, confines itself to the statement that Christ, by His one only oblation of Himself, made satisfaction for "our sins and those of all the faithful," and reconciled us to God.

NOTE 18, p. 55.

John Owen, *The Death of Death in the Death of Christ*, p. 274, vol. v. of his Collected Works [ed. 1826]. Baxter and Owen had a lively controversy on the methods and universality of redemption. The former writes as follows:—

"See therefore that you join no conceit of Christ which dishonoureth God... Many by mistaking the doctrine of Christ's intercession, do think of God the Father as one that is all wrath and justice, and unwilling of himself to be reconciled to man, and of the Second Person in the Trinity as more gracious and merciful, whose mediation abateth the wrath of the Father and with much ado maketh Him willing to have mercy on us. Whereas it is the love of God which is the original of our redemption, &c." Baxter, *Life of Faith*, ch. II. [Practical Works, ed. 1830, vol. 12, p. 189.] Baxter, however, goes on to deny that God needed to be reconciled to us, and thus lays himself open to Owen's strictures. See the latter's *Death of Christ, &c., cleared from the exceptions and objections of Mr. R. B.* Again, Baxter says (*ibid.* p. 190), "Some ... gather that God desired the sufferings of Christ as pleasing to Him in itself; as if He made a bargain with Christ to sell so much mercy to man, for so much blood and pains of Christ." Yet he looks upon Christ's death "as a convenient means to demonstrate God's justice and His holiness, and to vindicate the honour of His government and law," as well as "a warning to sinners not to sin presumptuously" (*ibid*). In his *Aphorisms of Justification* he accepts the ordinary doctrine of the time, that satisfaction was made to the Father's justice by Christ's endurance of what the law threatened. And he regards satisfaction, not as being strictly the payment of a debt (as is implied by the Scripture word λύτρον), but rather the offering to the Father an equivalent which He might accept if He would. See Thesis 7.

Note 19, p. 56.

See *Homiletic Magazine* for March 1883. Paper by the Right Rev. the Bishop of Amycla. The decree of the Council of Trent will be found in Session vi., ch. vii. and Canons x.–xiv.

Note 20, p. 57.

Appeal to all that doubt or disbelieve the Truths of the Gospel, ch. III. pp. 174–189 [3rd ed. 1778. Vol. VI. of Collected Works].

Note 21, p. 58.

Schleiermacher, *Der Christliche Glaube*, vol. II., sec. 101, 102. He distinguishes between Christ's *redeeming* and *atoning* activity. The first introduces believers into the power of His Divine Conscience; the second takes them into fellowship with His untroubled blessedness. But similar ideas as to the active and passive obedience of Christ, by the first of which He fulfilled the law of God, and by the second He endured the penalties for its non-fulfilment, were familiar enough to Divines of the Reformation period. See Note 16.

Note 22, p. 58.

Irving, *Doctrine of the Incarnation Opened*. Works, vol. v. p. 146. He says again (p. 147) that this theology is a "debtor and creditor theology."

Note 23, p. 58.

This is the Socinian view. See note on Lect. I.

Note 24, p. 58.

Maurice, *Theological Essays*, p. 147 (third edition). See also his *Doctrine of Sacrifice*.

Note 25, p. 61.

Godet's theory will be found in his *Études Bibliques: L'Œuvre de Jesus Christ*, pp. 143-194. Dr. McLeod Campbell's theory will be found in his treatise *On the Nature of the Atonement*, a most remarkable, original, and suggestive work. Its chief defects are, first, a singular obscurity of style, largely attributable, no doubt, to the greatness of the subject and the intense effort of the writer to do justice to it from a point of view entirely new, and next, an almost entire absence of any acquaintance with any but Puritan theology. We ought not to pass over a thoughtful work by the Rev. R. W. Dale, of Birmingham. His conclusions on the question are that Christ's Death was an Atonement. 1. Because it was a submission to, and acknowledgment of, the righteous Will of God. 2. Because it "rendered possible the retention or the recovery of our original and ideal relation to God through Christ" which sin had dissolved. 3. Because the death of Christ was the death of humanity to sin. 4. Because Christ's submission to God's law was a revelation of God's righteousness. Whatever may be thought of this explanation of the efficacy of Christ's sacrifice, it recognises the fact that that sacrifice was complex not simple in its action. And it also regards Christ's Death as a sacrifice for sin *on our behalf*—a suffering *for* us, and not merely "with" us, which, as Mr. Dale points out, Christ is never said to do in Holy Scripture, though we are frequently said to suffer with Him.

A recent instance of the failure of the ordinary theory to satisfy minds in general harmony with the school by which it is defended may be found in a treatise on the *Truth of God's Salvation*, by the Rev. C. F. Chase, Rector of St. Andrew by the Wardrobe (Hodder and Stoughton, 1880). The writer holds that "sin cannot be put away unless its penalty be paid" (p. 129). And again he says (p. 132), "As therefore the law was vindicated by its penalty being visited on Him whose dignity was the highest, so was it also vindicated in that He underwent its extremest measure." And yet (p. 190) he complains that men, by contending "that the sacrifice is effectual with God (for the purpose for which it is designed) because of the dignity of the offerer, or because of the infinite value of the offering," have "introduced into the Christian scheme the leading principle of the heathen system of sacrifice, in place of the leading system of the scriptural doctrine." "For the principle," he goes on (p. 191), "on which they explain the sacrifice of Christ is that it has influence with God to obtain the forgiveness of sin; not because of its efficacy to take away sin, but because of certain characteristics which God sees in the sacrifice." The distinction is not very clear; but Mr. Chase evidently feels that the Atonement should not be represented as an arbitrary arrangement, but that it should be in harmony with the Being of God, as well as the moral consciousness of mankind.

LECTURE IV.

NOTE 1, p. 69.

The whole force of the substitution theory is derived from the idea that "Justice requires that sin be punished because sin requires punishment." The idea is Anselm's (*Cur Deus Homo* I. 14); the words in which it is here expressed are those of Jonathan Edwards. This idea is the basis of all John Owen's elaborate reasoning. Of course, *if* the endurance of punishment be satisfaction for sin, there can be no disputing the soundness of this theory. But *is* it? Owen himself seems to have a momentary hesitation on the point when he declares (Collected Works, vol. v. p. 381) that the καταλλαγή or reconciliation "was accomplished δι' ἑνὸς δικαιώματος, by one *righteousness or* satisfaction, that is, of Christ." Is it not the fulfilment of the obedience man owed, rather than the endurance of the punishment man deserved, that is the centre of Christ's propitiatory work? This would naturally enough involve submission to the conditions in which fallen man had placed himself by sin. But this submission to those conditions, though a part, and a very necessary part, of the atoning work, ought not to be represented as the whole of it. We may profitably remember that Aristotle's definition of δικαίωμα (*Ethics*, v. 7) is the setting an unrighteous action right. This interpretation may be rejected by modern commentators under the influence of preconceived opinions. But it must be admitted that Aristotle understood his own language. And if his explanation of the word be accepted, then it is St. Paul's doctrine that our justification was effected, not by the simple endurance of punishment by Christ in our stead, but *by His setting right the wrong that we had done.*

Note 2, p. 72.

Professor Maurice, in his *Doctrine of Sacrifice,* p. 161, protests strongly against the "strange interpolation of the word *yet*" here. He does not seem to have observed that the fact of sin *does* bring justice and mercy into collision, at least until they are harmonised by the meeting of both in the Life and Death of Christ. We may believe that God "manifests His righteous will and purpose, His righteous character, in the death of His Son," but we may nevertheless see that the entrance of sin into the world has rendered it difficult for man to understand this righteous character, until Christ came to reveal it.

Note 3, p. 74.

St. Paul, in Rom. iii. 27, evidently considers that the πάρεσις or passing over of sins in the past constitutes a difficulty in the way of man's comprehension how God can be righteous.

Note 4, p. 75.

Anselm (*Cur Deus Homo,* Part II. ch. 11), says that if Jesus Christ had only paid God the tribute of obedience, He would have done no more than His duty. It was because He did more that He acquired His right to a reward, and claimed the whole human race as the equivalent for the price He had paid in enduring His awful Sufferings and Death. We may put the idea in another form, and say that had He obeyed the law for Himself only, had He not submitted to it as it affected all mankind, His Life would have been in no sense an Atonement for the sins of the world.

Note 5, p. 77.

We may observe how the views taken of the Sacrifice of Christ are conditioned by the spirit of the age. Anselm, in an age of despotic power, looks on punishment as the vindication of the authority and dignity of the sovereign. The sixteenth and seventeenth centuries brought us into contact with the idea of the duty of the chief magistrate to see that crime was properly punished. Hence the idea of strictly exacting the punishment due, or its equivalent. Our own more democratic age attaches more importance to the idea of vindicating the principle on which the law is founded. Submission to lawful authority will often, among ourselves, make punishment unnecessary. Let us observe for a moment how this vindication takes place. God pardons us fully, freely; as freely as if we had never sinned. But He does so on the condition that we shall concur fully in the reparation made on behalf of all men by His Beloved Son. Our hearts are to beat in unison with His. We are to regard submission to the great law of pain as our condemnation of the guilt of sin, the best acknowledgment we can make of God's justice in so dealing with it. We "bear about in our body the marks of the Lord Jesus," the *stigmata* He for ever affixed to sin. If our condemnation of sin be weak and ineffective, it gathers force from its association with His Who was alone able to brand it with the intensity it deserved. God pardons us because of our union in mind and spirit with Him Whose Mind was God's. Sin once condemned in this world in a manner that no man can mistake—sin once for all painted in its darkest, truest colours—there exists no reason henceforth why the Love of God should not flow out to man in all its fulness, why the gospel of free forgiveness should not be proclaimed to all mankind.

Note 6, p. 81.

The use of the words *redeem, redemption*, by the writers of the New Testament is by no means so precise as many suppose.

It is certainly not confined to the idea of making satisfaction to God's wrath or justice, and so securing to mankind immunity from punishment. Thus St. Peter (1 Pet. i. 18) speaks of our being redeemed from a vain conversation handed down from our ancestors, as though the result of this redemption were, not immunity from punishment, but holiness. St. Paul speaks of those under the law being "redeemed" that they might receive the adoption of sons (Gal. iv. 5). In Tit. ii. 14 he speaks of Christ as "redeeming us from all iniquity" ($\mathit{\dot{\alpha}νομία}$), and purifying us to Himself as a people of His own, zealous of good works. In another place (Rom. viii. 23) redemption and adoption are spoken of as synonymous. A remarkable expression is to be found in Eph. iv. 30. There our redemption is spoken of as a future process, and the Holy Spirit as being a seal setting us apart for the time when it should take place. So in Heb. xi. 35 it is used in the sense of deliverance from an evil fate. This is the sense in which the word is constantly used in the Old Testament. See Ps. xlix. 8, cvi. 10. It may be added that the word *Redeemer* is never once applied to Christ in the New Testament, but frequently to Jehovah in the Old. The term $\lambda υτρωτής$ is found in the New Testament. But it is applied to Moses.

Note 7, p. 84.

The allusion is to the story of Zaleucus, lawgiver of the Locrians, who had decreed that adulterers should lose the sight of both eyes. When his son was convicted of the crime, he ordered one of his own eyes and one of his son's to be put out, thus vindicating the authority of law, and yet manifesting his love for the offender. It is said that this combination of justice and mercy had such an effect on the Locrians, that while Zaleucus reigned over them no one was found guilty of adultery.

NOTE 8, p. 84.

See Keble, *Christian Year.* Hymn for Good Friday.

> Is it not strange, the darkest hour
> That ever dawned on sinful earth,
> Should touch the heart with softer power
> For comfort, than an angel's mirth?

NOTE 9, p. 86.

Another consideration may be added here. If, as the Fathers so constantly teach, Christ came to reverse by His Resurrection the sentence that man was doomed to corruption, and if He did so by overcoming the dominion of sin, He must enable us to overcome sin also. But since suffering is the natural and just consequence of sin, this victory must, in part at least, involve the teaching us how to endure suffering, how to bend the human will, which naturally shrinks from pain, to submission to those consequences, which, by God's Law, man's sin brings with it. And this equally whether the sin be our own or that of other men. How Christ did this by His Life, by His Agony, by His Death, needs no explanation.

NOTE 10, p. 87.

See the Biography of the Rev. Charles Lowder, who, however, is but one among many who have thus "laid down their lives for the brethren."

NOTE 11, p. 88.

" Which of us is there who does not feel that he has need of some expiation? There is something in the very bottom of each soul that bears witness to this his great want; a consciousness deeper than his deepest heart; yea, even if he had never heard of Christ it would be so. The soul instinctively turns to God, and every thought of Him must be accompanied with this feeling of alienation from Him and need of sacrifice; from a sense of what we are by nature, and what we are by frequent transgressions of the inward law. . . . But here we have all that the yearning heart could have desired supplied to us, and that accompanied with words and works and precepts of healing, compassion, and innumerable proofs of love beyond the thought of man." I. Williams, *Sermons on the Epistles and Gospels*, "The Great Sacrifice," pp. 357, 8. "It meets the inmost wants of the mind, it brings comfort to many a penitent soul when grief or trial, or the approach of death, has turned all beauty to ashes, all lower solaces into disgust and weariness." Abp. Thompson, *Bampton Lectures*, p. 132.

NOTE 12, p. 90.

A few supplementary observations may not be out of place here, in regard to one or two points which could not be treated in the Lectures.

1. Dr. McLeod Campbell insists very strongly on the importance of putting forth a view of the Atonement which shall satisfy, instead of doing violence to, the moral principles on which men are accustomed to act. And it is certain that the perusal of his pages, and the discovery that it is possible to account for Christ's sufferings and death on our account naturally, without any recourse to the supposition of an arbitrary arrangement, has given great relief to many minds. There is a feeling of spring and satisfaction in seeing how fully the fact of Christ's suffering on our behalf is in accordance with all our natural ideas of love and justice, instead of being contrary to them. That the popular mode of explaining Christ's Sacrifice does at first sight appear to conflict with those ideas, can hardly be denied. It is not immediately evident how the claims of natural justice are satisfied by the imputation of our sins to Christ, and of His righteousness to us, in consequence of His willingness to bear the punishment of our sins, although, no doubt, explana-

tions have been given which have considerably lessened the difficulty of the theory. There is a certain danger in the popular explanation. A creed which starts with a reversal of the ordinary principles of human morality, however much it may be justified by the argument that God's ways are not as our ways, has a tendency to unsettle the morality of those who accept it. If God be not just, men may argue, there is no reason why man should be so. And so it has come to pass that religion has too often been divorced from morality. The notion of our pardon being the result of a "device," an "arrangement," whereby God may be able to treat us as though we were innocent when we were not, has, again, led many to put off the conclusion of that arrangement till the last moment possible, and so to make the best of both worlds. But if we regard the Death of Christ as no "arrangement" or "transaction" of any kind, but a simple manifestation of the Mind of God towards sinners, and of the true attitude of man in the face of the evils sin has brought in its train, morality is not set aside, but rather encouraged. The whole character and career of Christ upon earth, from His Birth to His Death, is a proclamation of the oneness of God and man in regard to the fact of sin. Thus His life is one long manifestation of the fact that atonement, or reconciliation, which is the same thing, has been effected between God and man. The next point is, how are we to have a share in the reconciliation? The answer is, by sharing the Mind of Him Who made it. And if we ask how this is possible, we are told that it is by receiving His Perfect Life by a process of spiritual regeneration. If we further ask how this process is to be carried on, the reply is, it is begun and perfected in faith. Faith is the realization, the acknowledgment of spiritual facts (Heb. xi. 1). It involves perfect trust and confidence in God, in His goodness and love towards us, as well as His unchangeable aversion to all that is evil. It involves a full concurrence with His mind in all respects. This recognition of God as revealed in Jesus

NOTES TO LECTURE IV.

Christ, this acceptance of Him as the Incarnation of the Absolute Good, confers on us the power of disengaging ourselves from the bondage of sin, and of assimilating ourselves to His perfection. By it we "concur with all our hearts," as Godet says, with all that Christ has said and done. This "concurrence of heart," this "initial justification," leads by a natural consequence to a concurrence in fact. By union with the Perfect Man we attain at length to that mastery over sin, that perfect obedience to God, which, apart from Him, we never could have reached. The principle of Atonement thus formulated makes it clear why God's righteousness *must have* become ours if we have actually "received the Atonement," instead of being dangerously capable of being perverted into a reason why we should *not* "follow after righteousness," but on the contrary be contented with what has already been done for us. It becomes an incentive to morality, and not, as it has too often been made, an excuse for neglecting it.

2. Many of the ways of stating the doctrine of Atonement have involved the Arian or Nestorian or Eutychian heresy, or a combination of all three. For Christ has been spoken of as a different Being to the Father, or to God. His offering of Himself to bear our punishment has either been explained as though there were not only a distinction of Persons, but also of Mind and Purpose, between the Father and the Son; or it has been presented in such a way as to favour the idea that Jesus Christ was not Himself God,[1] or as though God the Word and the man Christ Jesus were two different Persons. We have to bear in mind (1) that the whole Mind, Will, and Purpose of the Persons in the Godhead is essentially and eternally one; and (2) that the mind of the man Christ Jesus and the mind of God are equally identical and impossible to be opposed one to the other. And thus Christ *could* only have manifested to us the Father's Will in His Life on earth. His sufferings *could* not have proceeded from any sense that He was the object of the

[1] As in Milton's *Paradise Lost*.

146   *NOTES TO LECTURE IV.*

Wrath of One to Whom He was eternally and indissolubly united. In fact we are compelled to give up the idea of suffering as any sign of God's Wrath against any person whatever (at least until sin has taken possession of his whole being), but simply as an indication of the fact of His determination to destroy sin. A doctrine, again, which would seem to impute passibility to the Godhead is either Eutychianism or worse. If, as some have thought, it were necessary that Christ should be God in order that His sufferings should be infinite in their intensity, then, surely, it were needful that God should suffer. But God is incapable of suffering,[1] and the manhood, it would seem, though united indissolubly to the Godhead in an Infinite Person, must yet remain itself finite, or else cease to be manhood altogether. The *communicatio idiomatum*, on which Cyril of Alexandria and his followers laid such stress in their opposition to Nestorianism, involved only the unity of the Person of Christ. It stopped short at that confusion of the attributes of the two *natures* which was condemned as Eutychianism. Thus, then, it would appear doubtful whether the sufferings of Christ *were* infinite; at least sufficiently doubtful to make it very unwise to frame a theory of the Atonement which depends entirely on the hypothesis that they were so.

3. It is as well to assert distinctly, in conclusion, that the doctrine of an objective reconciliation of God to man and man to God through the Death of Christ has never been denied or questioned in these pages. "Christ suffered for our sins, the just for the unjust," yet not that He might relieve us from all punishment, not that He might bear the Father's wrath or

[1] I have said (Lect. iv. p. 84), "God has suffered." This is not incompatible with the orthodox doctrine, by reason of the union of the Godhead and Manhood in one Person in Jesus Christ. But to speak of God as becoming man in order to give man an "infinite capacity for suffering," implies surely that the *Godhead* has suffered, which is contrary to the universal teaching of the Christian Church concerning God. The same objection, however, does not apply to the statement that God became man in Christ in order to give infinite *value* to His sufferings.

satisfy the claims of His justice by suffering in our stead, but that He *might bring* or *lead us to God*, Whom our transgressions had alienated. By the sufferings and Death of the sinless One, God and man were reconciled. This is the fact which Scripture proclaims. With this fact let us be content; let each man explain it as he can. As Mr. Dale ably says in his *Lectures on the Atonement*, already quoted (p. 4): "It is not the doctrine of the Death of Christ that atones for human sin, but the Death itself; and great as are the uses of the doctrine in promoting the healthy and vigorous development of the spiritual life, the Death of Christ has such a wonderful power, that it inspires faith in God, and purifies the heart, though the doctrine of the Atonement may be unknown or denied." We may hope that many are not strangers to the power of Christ's Sacrifice who are yet far from comprehending the method of its efficacy. But that the Death of Christ is a death unto sin in all those who strive to reflect its spirit; that by union of heart and soul with that One Perfect Sacrifice for sin can peace of mind and forgiveness alone be attained, that we are "reconciled to God by the Death of Christ, saved by His Life," are truths to which the salvation of every Christian soul must ultimately be traced, let his present opinion concerning them be what it may.

SELECT PRESS NOTICES

OF

THE FIRST EDITION OF THIS VOLUME.

The Scotsman.

In the Hulsean Lectures for 1883-4, Mr. Lias has undertaken to show that the evangelistical theory of the *Atonement*, involving the doctrine that Jesus Christ substituted Himself in the place of sinners, and in their stead bore the wrath and curse of God due to sin—a theory which "has been insisted upon as the very key-stone of the Christian faith," and the rejection of which "has frequently been regarded, both by supporters and opponents of Christianity, as the rejection of revealed religion"—was not propounded by the first preachers of the Gospel, nor by their successors for the next fifteen hundred years, and that it is not accepted by the vast majority of Christians of our own day. His precise position is this :—

"It is not my purpose to controvert this doctrine. If it bring satisfaction and comfort to any man, far be it from me to deprive him of this satisfaction. But there are minds to which this doctrine not only brings no satisfaction or comfort whatever, but it causes them the utmost perplexity and disquiet—nay, it even drives them to reject the whole Gospel of Christ. The question therefore arises, not whether this explanation be in itself a rational and tenable explanation of the language of Holy Scripture on this high and mysterious subject, but whether it be the only rational and tenable explanation of that language."

Accordingly, he sets himself, in his second lecture, to examine the Scriptural teaching on the subject, and arrives at the conclusion that the theory in question, although not directly negatived by the teaching of Christ and His Apostles, is only an inference, and by no means a necessary inference, from certain texts. He finds that the writers of the New Testament "represent the Lord's death, not in one, but in various aspects," and that, among all their statements, "there is not one single passage which explicitly asserts that it derived its reconciling power from its being the bearing the Divine wrath for sin in our stead " In a word, according to Mr. Lias, the evangelical theory of the Atonement may pass "as a possible explanation, or contribution towards an explanation, of a stupendous mystery," but ought neither to be imposed nor accepted "as a fundamental article of faith." Those who hold it, therefore, "have no right to impugn the orthodoxy of those who resort to other explanations of the Lord's propitiatory work." In the third lecture, he examines the various theories of propitiation which have been propounded in the Christian Church since the time of the Apostles; and in the fourth, he reviews the various aspects of propitiation which are either presented or suggested in Scripture. The work, written throughout in calm, earnest, and temperate language, and in a candid spirit, is the result of considerable thought and research; and is well fitted to deepen the impression, already widespread among thoughtful men, that the framers of our Creeds, both ancient and modern, have erred in attempting to formulate and define doctrines which, as presented in Scripture, are vague, mysterious, and incomprehensible.

The Church Quarterly.

The value of the volume before us must not be estimated by its size. Mr. Lias has succeeded in compressing into less than one hundred and fifty pages an immense amount of material, and we cordially recommend his work as containing an admirable summary and excellent introduction to larger works treating of the vast subject with which it deals. . . . But the special claim which the writer has upon our gratitude is raised by the manner in which he has dealt with modern difficulties. . . . Doubts, we know, are sometimes driven in, and seated the firmer through want of sympathy on the part of those to whom they are expressed. Mr. Lias, though he is strong, or rather *because* he is strong in his own position, is ready to give a patient hearing to those who are troubled in mind, and is willing to examine afresh with them the great mystery of the Atonement, in the hope that by so doing he may remove some of their misgivings and misconceptions. . . . This is clearly the right method to employ. . . . It is a work which might well be placed in the hands of those who are themselves troubled and perplexed.

Altogether Mr. Lias has produced a really helpful introduction to the study of a subject of overwhelming importance, and has uttered a well-timed protest against the narrowness of so much popular teaching and the defective character of many modern theories.

The Banner.

Those who already know other works by Mr. Lias, such as the Commentaries on the Book of Judges and on the Epistles to the Corinthians in the *Cambridge Bible for Schools*, and the introduction to the Book of Joshua in the *Pulpit Commentary*, will be prepared to find sober and solid results in these lectures; and they will not be disappointed. The volume is a small one, and we trust will prove attractive to some, to whom such works as Oxenham's *History of the Catholic Doctrine of the Atonement*, or Archbishop Thomson's *Bampton Lectures*, might seem too formidable. It supplies a real want. There are very many people who, when the subject comes before them in Scripture, in sermons, or in articles of periodicals, feel that their ideas on this difficult subject are vague and unsatisfactory. If any one ask them point-blank for their view of the Atonement, they would probably find it hard, even with the best will to comply with the request, to give any definite answer. Still less, if the difficulty which attends the ordinary Protestant account of the doctrine were urged upon them, would they be able to show how the difficulty may be met. These lectures will give considerable help in both cases. They will help those whose notions on the subject are misty and ill-defined to attain to something more clear and definite: and still more they will convince persons whose minds are perplexed by the common manner of expounding the doctrine that it is quite possible to hold fast the doctrine without committing oneself to the difficulties involved in the ordinary exposition. In doing this Mr. Lias has done a large number of thoughtful Christians a very real service.

The Aberdeen Journal.

A very modest reason is assigned by Mr. Lias for the publication of his lectures: namely, that "it seems likely that a short introduction to the study of the doctrine on which they treat might be useful to the theological student before entering on larger works." A "certain theory of atonement," he goes on to say in his Preface, "which, though by no means excluded by the language of Scripture, is not laid down in Scripture itself, has been insisted upon as the very keystone of the Christian faith. The rejection of this theory has frequently been regarded both by supporters and opponents of Christianity as the rejection of revealed religion. The object of these lectures is to show that there is no ground whatever for such a supposition; that the theory in question was not propounded by the first preachers of the Gospel, nor by their successors for the next fifteen hundred years, and that it is not accepted by the vast majority of Christians of our own time. Consequently a man may be a very good Christian without believing it, and a very serious hindrance in the way of belief is at once removed." The theory here referred to is the substitution theory associated with the great names of St. Augustine and Calvin, and in more modern times with such writers as Dr. Owen, President Edwards, and Dr. Chalmers. And Mr. Lias says, " The question arises, whether it be possible to hold firmly to the truth that Jesus Christ was a true and proper sacrifice for sin ; that we were redeemed, saved, and justified by His Blood ; that on the cross He offered Himself as a full, perfect, and sufficient sacrifice, oblation, and satisfaction for the sins of the whole world ; that He bare the sins of the whole world ; that He bare our sins in His own Body on the tree, without being compelled to acknowledge that all this was effected by His having borne the wrath of God against sin, or an exact equivalent to it, in our stead ; that it was His having borne the punishment of our sins which satisfied the insulted dignity of the Father, paid the penalty inexorably demanded by His justice, and so enabled Him to lay His wrath aside." "If then," he goes on to say, "we can show that it is not the Scripture doctrine of propitiation that is at fault, but that the centre of gravity of the Christian scheme has been shifted by modern theories of the Atonement, if we can show that satisfaction to Divine justice has taken the place of the restoration of the Divine in fallen man, that the doctrine of propitiation rests upon that of Christ's Godhead, and not Christ's Godhead upon the necessity of exacting an adequate penalty either from the offender or his subtitute, if we can persuade men that Christ's incarnation, not His death, has been from the first the pivot upon which the Gospel scheme has revolved, we may perhaps do something to restore that faith which has so unhappily been lost." After noticing the objections of Socinus, Priestley, Carpenter, Martineau, and W. R. Greg, and the admission of the force of such objections by certain divines of the Anglican Church—Magee, Jowett, Maurice, &c—he goes on, in his second lecture, to give the Scripture teaching regarding Propitiation. In the third, he gives the theories of the Propitiation that have been held in the Church, from Clement of Rome to Bushnell, M'Leod, Campbell, and Godet ; and in the fourth, the various aspects of Propitiation. To the lectures, which cover ninety pages, there is appended fifty-seven pages of notes. Notwithstanding its small size, perhaps partly on account of its smallness, this is one of the most satisfactory and valuable contributions to the literature of the subject which has been published in recent times.

The Saturday Review.

Mr. Lias explains, in the preface to his Hulsean Lectures on *The Atonement*, that the volume is designed as an introduction for theological students "before entering on larger works, such as Oxenham's *Catholic Doctrine of the Atonement*, the article in Herzog's *Encyclopædia*, Archbishop Thompson's *Bampton Lectures*," and some other works he mentions. And he is anxious to insist that "a certain theory of Atonement," frequently represented both by the supporters and opponents of Christianity as part and parcel of revealed religion, was never heard of before the Reformation, and is still rejected by the vast majority of Christians, meaning apparently the Lutheran view of "imputation." His aim is to prove, by reference to New Testament teaching, and the development of doctrine in the Church, that the received Protestant theories of substitution and satisfaction are—not necessarily untrue, though he pretty plainly implies his own disbelief of them, but—entirely open questions, not binding on orthodox believers either by the authority of Scripture or of the Catholic Church.

The Record.

Mr. Lias's book is really a somewhat plausible but not the less dangerous attack on the doctrine of substitution. Again, respecting the Old Testament root *caphar*, which in some form or other invariably stands behind our word "atonement" in the earlier Scriptures, Mr. Lias says, "It is nowhere intimated that this (atonement) takes place by the substitution of a victim to bear the punishment of the offender." Substitution, in short, was not the meaning of the Old Testament sacrifices. We wonder what was. There is one difficulty raised by Mr. Lias's book with which we cannot but sympathise in great measure. The atonement has been often expounded in such a way that a metaphysical question is met by a moral answer. It may be true, and if we accept the teaching of the Sacred Scriptures, it is undeniable, that the outraged and broken law of God requires life for life. But God's moral laws are only another side of His natural laws in all cases where we are able to investigate them. What is the natural side of the law of substitution in the atonement? It may not be possible for us to answer this question perfectly in this life. But it is at least possible to recognise its existence, and it is also possible to avoid inadequate and unsatisfactory replies. We may not deny the doctrine of substitution on the one side, nor on the other must we presume to estimate the value of our Lord's infinite sacrifice by the number of souls whom it saves. Nor again, does it seem to us quite reverent or consistent with the Divine character as revealed in Scripture, to say that God would have required life for life in order to satisfy His offended majesty, if the laws of His own will or creation had permitted Him to save man in any other way. It is because we are even His offspring "that He must die to save us." The Divine purpose in our creation determined the nature of our being and probation. The nature of our being and probation gave shape to the results of the fall. The results of the fall demanded the process of restoration. In fact, He who made us could only redeem us by taking our nature and dying for us. It is as idle to say He did not do so as it is presumptuous to explain fully why the thing was necessary to be done.

LONDON : J. NISBET & CO., 21 BERNERS STREET.

NISBET'S
THEOLOGICAL LIBRARY.

Nisbet's Theological Library.

THE ATONEMENT:

A Symposium.

By Archdeacon FARRAR, D.D., Professor ABRAHAMS, Rev. Dr. LITTLEDALE, Rev. G. W. OLVER, Principal RAINY, D.D., the BISHOP OF AMYCLA, and others.

Crown 8vo, 6s.

"We recommend our readers to purchase the work. Although the papers are naturally argumentative and not devotional, the record of the efforts of different minds to grasp the doctrine of the Atonement cannot but be helpful."—*Literary Churchman.*

INSPIRATION:

A Symposium on In what Sense and within what Limits is the Bible the Word of God?

By Archdeacon FARRAR, the Revs. Principal CAIRNS, Professor STANLEY LEATHES, D.D., and others.

Crown 8vo, 6s.

"The volume is an interesting one, written throughout in a temperate and scholarly spirit, and likely to prove useful to the higher stamp of theological students."—*Church Times.*

IMMORTALITY:

A Symposium on What are the Foundations of the Belief in the Immortality of Man?

By the Rev. Prebendary Row, M.A., Rabbi HERMANN ADLER, Professor G. G. STOKES, F.R.S., Rev. Canon KNOX-LITTLE, Rev. EDWARD WHITE, and others.

Crown 8vo, 6s.

"A work of great and absorbing interest, marked by extreme ability."—*Literary Churchman.*

Nisbet's Theological Library—*continued*.

THE PATRIARCHAL TIMES.

By the Rev. THOMAS WHITELAW, D.D.

Crown 8vo, 6s.

"The essays form individually and as a whole an articulated chain of reasoning, the charm of which consists in the fact, that having presented to the reader a convincing conclusion, it leaves him in a state of wonder that he had never arrived there on his own account."—*Record*.

FUTURE PROBATION:

A Symposium on the Question, "Is Salvation Possible after Death?"

By the Rev. STANLEY LEATHES, D.D., Principal J. CAIRNS, D.D., LL.D., Rev. EDWARD WHITE, Rev. STOPFORD BROOKE, M.A., Rev. Dr. LITTLEDALE, Right Rev. the BISHOP OF AMYCLA, &c.

Crown 8vo, 6s.

"This volume deals with a subject of profound and awful moment, and the papers as a whole are written with considerable ability."—*Literary Churchman*.

"To men afflicted with the 'malady of thought' this book will prove delightful reading; and to men not so afflicted, we hope it will carry the infection."—*Irish Ecclesiastical Gazette*.

ZECHARIAH:

HIS VISIONS AND HIS WARNINGS.

By the Rev. W. LINDSAY ALEXANDER, D.D.

Crown 8vo, 6s.

"Those who have found difficulty in grasping the brief and mysterious parables of the Hebrew Prophet, will derive great help in their study of this prophecy from Dr. Alexander's careful and painstaking discussion."—*Literary Churchman*.

"The exposition of the Prophet's meaning in reference to his own age is sober and sound; and the bearing of the writing upon the Church in all ages, and the spiritual import of the imagery and the history, are excellently brought out and illustrated."—*Church Bells*.

Nisbet's Theological Library—*continued*.

DANIEL I.—VI.:
AN EXPOSITION OF THE HISTORICAL PORTIONS OF THE WRITINGS OF THE PROPHET DANIEL.

By the Very Rev. R. PAYNE SMITH, D.D., Dean of Canterbury.

Crown 8vo, 6s.

"These papers are of sterling value, and cover much ground that is imperfectly known, or not known at all, even by Biblical students who are not, so to speak, specialists in this department of antiquities. No one could possibly read this volume without adding greatly to their knowledge of this important prophecy."—*Literary Churchman*.

"The author keeps the spiritual element constantly before the mind, and brings out in a most natural and interesting manner many useful lessons that are latent in the narrative."—*Record*.

FOUR CENTURIES OF SILENCE;
OR, FROM MALACHI TO CHRIST.

By the Rev. R. A. REDFORD, M.A., LL.B., Professor of Systematic Theology and Apologetics, New College, London.

Crown 8vo, 6s.

"Carefully and intelligently done. The critical views expressed appear to us generally just. His account of Philo is particularly good."—*Literary Churchman*.

THE FIRST EPISTLE OF ST. JOHN:
AN EXPOSITION WITH HOMILETICAL TREATMENT.

By the Rev. J. J. LIAS, M.A.

7s. 6d.

"One of the most beautiful, instructive, and edifying expositions of St. John's First Epistle we have ever seen. Mr. Lias seems to us to have entered into the very heart of St. John's Divine Theology. We know of no book that throws more light upon the teaching of the Apostle whom Jesus loved. It responds to some of the holiest aspirations of the Christian soul."—*Methodist Times*.

"There are some good things in the volume which (so far as our knowledge reaches) are not to be found elsewhere."—*Classical Review*.

Nisbet's Theological Library—*continued.*

THE FIRST LETTER OF PAUL THE APOSTLE TO TIMOTHY:

A POPULAR COMMENTARY.

With a Series of Forty Sermonettes.

By ALFRED ROWLAND, LL.B., B.A. (Lond.)

Crown 8vo, 6s.

"An admirable example of what a Commentary intended for general use should be. The sermonettes are full of pointed, earnest, devout applications of the sacred text to the circumstances of every-day life."—*Christian World Pulpit.*

NON-BIBLICAL SYSTEMS OF RELIGION.

By Archdeacon FARRAR, D.D., Canon RAWLINSON, Rev. W. WRIGHT, D.D., Rabbi G. J. EMANUEL, B.A., Sir WILLIAM MUIR, and others.

Extra crown 8vo, 6s.

"The men who have written upon the various departments of the book are among the most capable, and what they have stated is likely to prove not only interesting, but of the highest value to the cause of religion."—*Christian Commonwealth.*

CHRISTIANITY AND EVOLUTION:

MODERN PROBLEMS OF THE FAITH.

By the Revs. G. MATHESON, D.D., T. FOWLE, M.A., Sir GEORGE W. COX, M.A., Professor MOMERIE, LL.D., and others.

Extra crown 8vo, 6s.

"Each writer takes up a distinct side of this subject, and treats it always intelligently, sometimes with really striking ability and acuteness."—*Literary Churchman.*

"All the essays are eminently readable, and some of them are of the deepest interest. They contain a vast amount of valuable information for the general reader in the shape of well-digested results from an enormous mass of reading."—*Public Opinion.*

Nisbet's Theological Library—*continued.*

THE CHRISTIAN FULFILMENTS AND USES OF THE LEVITICAL SIN-OFFERING.

By the Rev. HENRY BATCHELOR.

Extra crown 8vo, 5s.

"As the minute and learned investigations of Kurz conducts to the result that the Israelitish sin-offering was penal and vicarious, so does Mr. Batchelor furnish more easily mastered proof of the same truth. His work is admirable so far as it goes."—*British Weekly.*

"The style is terse, vigorous, and scholarly, and will be read by all who believe in the old-fashioned Gospel with pleasure and profit."—*Life of Faith.*

THE MENTAL CHARACTERISTICS OF OUR LORD JESUS CHRIST.

By the Rev. H. N. BERNARD, M.A., LL.B.

Extra crown 8vo, 6s.

"So to treat the purely human side of Christ's compound nature as not to leave out of sight the divine powers of which He must have been conscious of possessing, even when He did not will to call them into action, was evidently a task requiring considerable care, considerable skill in handling the nicer points of divinity, and perhaps some logical dexterity; and Mr. Bernard, so far as we can pretend to judge, seems to tread this perilous path with a firm step, and with a successful avoidance of heritical pit-falls on one side or the other."—*Scotsman.*

LONDON: J. NISBET & CO., 21 BERNERS STREET.

www.ingramcontent.com/pod-product-compliance
Lightning Source LLC
Chambersburg PA
CBHW031447160426
43195CB00010BB/881